# Project Bosporus

M.I.T.
Student
System
Project

M.I.T. Report No. 21

# PROJECT BOSPORUS

City and Port of Boston (Cape Cod in the Background)
Photograph by Aerial Photos of New England, Boston

M.I.T. Report No. 21

# PROJECT BOSPORUS

## Boston Port Utilization Study

**Interdepartmental Student Project in Systems Engineering
at the Massachusetts Institute of Technology, Spring Term, 1968**

David F. Cahn, Project Manager
Anthony J. Aliberti, Assistant Project Manager
Professor William W. Seifert and Kathryn N. Corones, Editors

**The M.I.T. Press**
Massachusetts Institute of Technology
Cambridge, Massachusetts, and London, England

FOREWORD

This volume is the end product in another of a series of efforts carried on under the subject "Special Studies in Systems Engineering" which is designed to engage upperclassmen and graduate students from a number of different departments in a coordinated investigation of a complex problem of considerable current interest.

The effort is compressed into a single term of approximately fourteen weeks and, for the class as a whole, culminates in a formal presentation offered to a select group of individuals who have special interest in the specific project under consideration or in the educational process involved. The project statement provided at the beginning of the term is purposely broad in order to force the students to ask penetrating questions relative to the over-all goals to be achieved and finally to establish specific subgoals to which individuals or small groups may direct attention. The effort required to define specific objective necessarily is time consuming and detracts from that which might be spent on detailed analyses of specifics. None the less, the faculty involved in this effort believe this trade-off is appropriate in as much as students spend the greatest part of their time studying relatively narrow issues in considerable depth and have little opportunity to take a broad view of complex problems. Furthermore, we believe that the future will have increasing need for persons trained to take the broader view and willing and anxious to work as part of a team.

Our goal has been to make an edited version of the results of each study available within six months to a year after the oral presentation of a project. Unfortunately, this particular effort was considerably delayed for a number of reasons. Still, the problems of Boston's air and seaports remain as acute today as they were in 1968. We hope that making this report available may bring some new insight to these problems and thereby assist somewhat in their ultimate resolution.

William W. Seifert
Professor of Electrical Engineering
Professor of Engineering
 in Civil Engineering
Massachusetts Institute of Technology

Cambridge, Massachusetts
June, 1970

# TABLE OF CONTENTS

Table of Contents

# LIST OF ILLUSTRATIONS

# List of Illustrations

# LIST OF TABLES

PREFACE

Project BOSPORUS is the product of an interdisciplinary subject
having the specific title "Special Studies in Systems Engineering", which
was offered under the general direction of Professor William W. Seifert of
M.I.T.'s School of Engineering in the Spring of 1968. The term "Systems
Engineering" has a wide variety of connotations depending upon who is using
it and what his specific purposes are. We can define our use of the term by
quoting from the Preface of the report on Project ROMULUS, which was
carried on a year earlier.

"For our purposes, then, systems engineering is no more than
the judicious juxtaposition of ideas and the simultaneous, parallel
consideration and interaction of these ideas toward a common goal."

The specific problem addressed in Project BOSPORUS was identified
in the problem statement circulated to prospective enrollees prior to the
beginning of the term. The content of that statement is as follows:

DESIGN OF AIRPORT AND SEAPORT FACILITIES FOR BOSTON

A number of agencies are currently examining a variety of problems associated with the Boston Harbor region. The Harbor is a potentially beautiful and valuable resource which still remains substantially underdeveloped. Shipping activity in the port has been declining steadily, while traffic growth at Logan Airport will outstrip facilities before many years. No one has yet undertaken a sufficiently comprehensive study of the region, analyzing optimal locations for sea and air traffic terminals and coordinated development of remaining areas.

Numerous possibilities for redevelopment of the waterfront, the port facilities, and the Harbor Islands have been discussed by public and private agencies and in the press. It is proposed that the class appraise the potential demand which the New England Region might generate for ocean shipping if a suitable modern port were developed and study where such a port might be located, if a demand for it exists. Included with this may be some investigation of proposals for redevelopment of existing dock areas in East Boston.

A joint and related study should be made of the present projections of air traffic growth, both passenger and air cargo. It has been predicted that a new airport facility will be needed for Boston by the year 1975. The specific requirements imposed on the new site if it is to handle the SST and Jumbo size aircraft must be

investigated. Runway and terminal requirements and noise factors,
air space utilization and possible conflicts in air traffic control
with existing airports all need to be considered in selecting the
new site and in developing a comprehensive airport plan.

One of the interesting possibilities is the integration of the
seaport and airport in such a manner that they can jointly use some
of the same ground transportation systems and terminal and storage
facilities. The feasibility of such a combined facility shall be
investigated in depth, with a final report on the advantages and
disadvantages of such a combination. This is to be compared to
alternative locations for either the seaport or the airport.

While the specific topics to be included depend on the interests and backgrounds of the student participants, the following list
is illustrative (but not exhaustive) of the kinds of topics that might
be involved.

Possibility of a Second Airport
    Traffic Requirements
    Location Possibilities
    Design Concepts and Potential
Seaport Development
    Potential Demand
    Location
    Quality Characteristics
    Possible Design Integration with Airport
Redesign of Harbor Area
    New Uses for Areas Possibly Vacated by Removal of
        Sea and Air Terminals
    Ocean and Coastal Engineering Aspects of Proposed Changes
    Integration of Multiple Uses
Ground Transport
    Access to Harbor Facilities

Special Innovations for Terminal Access
Improved Freight Handling
Effect on Current Boston Traffic Patterns
Political and Social Consequences
New Neighborhoods
Changes in Political Divisions
Jurisdictional Clarification
Financial Support
Finance Plans -- Public and Private
Benefit Assessment
Anticipated Revenues
Management of Planning and Implementation
Enabling Legislation
Political Structures
Publicity and Public Acceptance

This subject is designed for graduate students and selected seniors from throughout the Schools of Engineering, Architecture and Planning, and Humanities and Social Science, and Management. Guest lecturers from industry, government, and universities will develop some of the fundamental issues relating to the project.

The students themselves will be responsible for the internal organization of the subject, including leadership, as well as design teams and subgroups to concentrate on specific aspects of the problem, while the faculty and staff will be available as consultants. Some groups, for instance, would develop the requirements for port, air-port, housing and recreational facilities, others the technical aspects of facilities construction and others yet the political and organizational procedures involved in such an undertaking. As in previous years, the students will be responsible for producing an integrated plan and making a public presentation thereof at the end of the academic year. This presentation, along with a publishable report, are the culmination of the semester's efforts.

The make-up of the group which carried on this study is shown in Table P.1.

| Participating Student | Departmental Affiliation | Year |
|---|---|---|
| Leonid Afanasieff | Naval Architecture | G |
| Anthony J. Aliberti | Mechanical Engineering | 4 |
| Ernest W. Ascherman | Mechanical Engineering | G |
| David R. Berry | Mechanical Engineering | 4 |
| James E. Bodamer | Mechanical Engineering | G |
| Ronald P. Burd | Mechanical Engineering | 4 |
| David F. Cahn | Mechanical Engineering | 4 |
| Joshua D. Coran | Mechanical Engineering | 4 |
| Cheryl A. Cretin | Mechanical Engineering | 4 |
| Gene E. Fax | Naval Architecture | G |
| Paul A. Forbes | Mechanical Engineering | 4 |
| Paul M. Goldberg | Sloan School of Management | G |
| Brooks Hilliard | Mechanical Engineering | 4 |
| David Hoover | Sloan School of Management | G |
| Jeffrey S. Horowitz | Mechanical Engineering | G |
| Mohammad A. Jan | City and Regional Planning | G |
| James E. Just | Electrical Engineering | 4 |
| Joseph Kleinmann | Mechanical Engineering | 4 |
| Aaron Lehmann | Naval Architecture | G |
| Robert S. MacDonald | Mechanical Engineering | 4 |
| Frank A. March | Naval Architecture | G |
| Jerome E. Milch | Political Science | G |
| Edward H.E. Nabbe | Naval Architecture | G |
| Raul Nino-Guerrero | City and Regional Planning | G |
| William E. Onorato | Political Science | 4 |
| Thomas R. Rice | Mechanical Engineering | G |
| Ronald B. Rosenfeld | Mathematics | 3 |
| Robert H. Sturges, Jr. | Mechanical Engineering | 4 |
| Paul Sullivan | Harvard Law School | G |
| William B. Zimmerman | Mechanical Engineering | 4 |

Table P.1 Enrollment in "Special Studies in Systems Engineering"

The students were encouraged to assume the greatest possible responsibility for the actual development of this project. None the less,

a large group of faculty made themselves available to provide advice and

consultation. Those who participated most actively are listed in Table P.2.

| Faculty Member | Departmental Affiliation |
| --- | --- |
| Professor D.M.B. Baumann | Mechanical Engineering |
| Dr. S.M. Breuning | Project TRANSPORT, Coordinator |
| Professor J. Clarkeson | Civil Engineering |
| Professor F.C. Colcord, Jr. | Political Science |
| Professor R.H. Cross, III | Civil Engineering |
| Professor R.L. deNeufville | Civil Engineering |
| Professor E.G. Frankel | Naval Architecture and Marine Engineering |
| Mr. P.B. Herr | City and Regional Planning |
| Mr. S.M. Jacks | Sloan School of Management |
| Mr. A. Kettaneh | Project TRANSPORT |
| Professor W.W. Seifert | Electrical Engineering, Professor in Charge |
| Professor R.W. Simpson | Aeronautics and Astronautics |

Table P.2 Faculty

The students are, of course, the ones who deserve credit for the actual

ideas presented in this report. Special note should be given to David Cahn,

who served as over-all student project manager, and to Anthony Aliberti, who

drafted portions of this report. Finally, major credit for the fact that his report

was finally brought into publishable form is due to Kathryn Corones, who

drafted some sections from fragmentary student notes, edited the entire manu-

script, prepared the index, and even typed the copy from which the final report

was reproduced. Without her quiet but effective prodding and personal efforts,

this document would never have been completed.

June, 1970                                                          William W. Seifert

Chapter 1

DESIGN OVERVIEW

## 1.1    The Area of Concern

One generally defines Greater Boston as the area within Route
128's circumference. In a study of Boston as a port, however, the entire
New England region figures, for Boston serves as a transfer point for
many long-haul passenger and freight movements bound for a final extra-
city destination (Figure 1.1). In the widest sense, the functioning of
Boston's ports affects the entire nation.

In responding to these realities, we relied upon an awareness
of national and regional economic and social trends. Yet our primary
clients were the people and communities which would directly feel
changes in the physical port or port policies. The intensity of our study
reached its maximum focus at the sites we planned to develop; of central
concern were the communities and districts neighboring these sites.

The airport and seaport of Boston commanded our primary attention.
Each suffers, the airport from overcrowding and inefficiency which will
worsen as national demand continues to soar, the seaport from obsolete

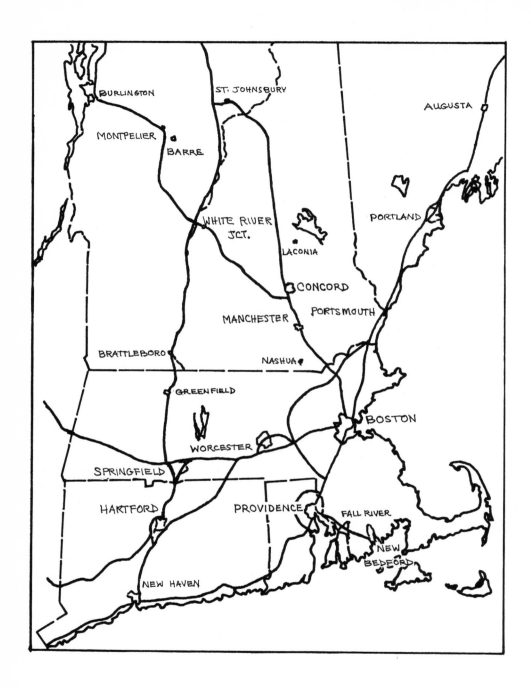

Figure 1.1  New England

methods and a resulting wane in traffic. The two facilities presently operate

in almost uniform independence; we sought areas to consolidate, both in

regard to physical facilities and management policies, so that one design

interlocking plans for each port might create a fine total port.

### 1.2    Airport Problems

Commercial jets can fly at speeds greater than 600 m.p.h., yet we

do not speak of a twenty minute trip from Boston to New York. Failure to

realize the airplane's potential speed capability stems from two basic

problems: the present system cannot handle the magnitude of current travel

demand; appropriate technological advances have not been made in certain

vital components of the total system. As a result of the first problem,

passengers experience pre-flight waits due to traffic in preceding ports,

long delays before becoming airborne because one's own port of departure

is congested, and lengthy in-flight circling above one's overtaxed destina-

tion. Due to the second, they must tolerate large home-to-port access times

because of overburdened highways and/or distant airports, and delays

because of slow terminal transactions. Together these two problems spell

an inefficiency, a loss of passenger time, that a truly all-weather capability

and improved vehicles and operational procedures would but slightly

alleviate.

Furthermore, the air industry afflicts those indifferent to its services,

those beyond its boundaries. Airports generate traffic; cars clog local roads.

Preferred flight times coincide with business rush hours; highway congestion is augmented. Jet aircraft make noise. Offensive noise levels from jet

aircraft are detected up to three miles on either side of flight paths.

Jet engines contribute 2 to 4% of all air pollutants to the city.

By 1971, long-range, fixed-wing aircraft, carrying nearly five

hundred passengers, will be in service. This leap in jetcraft technology -

the jet is already the best designed, the most efficient single element

of the system - increases our apprehension about future air service. A

single jumbo-jet touch-down could involve 1,000 passengers (500 arriving

at the airport, and 500 departing), 2,000 pieces of luggage, scores of

relatives, friends, greeters, and well-wishers, all to be properly handled

within the short turn-around time desired by the airlines. Ground transport

for these people alone, for this one flight alone, could involve over 1,000

automobiles or 200 buses or one full-length train. Late on a summer after-

noon, an airport such as Logan or J.F.K. may be expected to handle,

simultaneously, several superjets and numerous smaller commercial air-

craft, as well as the usual covey of private planes. Response to passenger

demand will soon place an immense burden on our airports which will not

be lightened without new methods of passenger and baggage handling,

new means for providing access to the airport and new airport configurations.

To make specific recommendations, we focus an investigation on

one city and its airport: Logan Airport in Boston[1]. The site Logan International

---

[1] Logan Airport is the 8th busiest in the world.

Airport now occupies was never chosen as a good airport location; rather,

the area has gradually developed since September 8, 1923, from a small

flying field to the present 2,200 acre Logan Airport complex, with its four

runways (a fifth is under construction), a multitude of terminal facilities,

and a partially completed $175 million expansion program.

Although Logan lies within four miles of the major commercial,

population, and industrial centers of the city, it is not close in terms of

time. To reach Logan, the majority of users must cross the harbor via

either the Mystic Bridge or the Callahan Tunnel, plus the Central Artery.

In the morning and afternoon rush hours, when most flights leave, the

main arteries overfill, slowing traffic. One study[2] has predicted a rush

hour trip from the airport to any of the major city centers of 60 to 70

minutes by 1980. Industrial and population centers also currently appear

to be expanding in the outer rings of 128 and I-495 and to the south and

west of the core city. In time, the location of Boston's only major air-

port on the north side of the city will prove an even more acute problem.

Proximity of the airport in terms of audibility, however, cannot

be denied. Large residential areas are presently subjected to high noise

levels. These include the communities of East Boston, South Boston,

Winthrop, and Revere, all in the direct line of one or more of the airport

flight paths. Residents and public officials in each of these adjoining

_____

[2] Munds, Allan J., Ground Access to Major Airports in the United States,
   Flight Transportation Laboratory Report FTL-R68-7, M.I.T., Cambridge,
   Mass., January 1969.

communities have complained vociferously about the noise and have

effectively prevented the expansion of the port.

In addition, because Logan is bounded by the major shipping

channels to the West, and by East Boston to the East, current runway

construction cannot be expanded without difficulty and expense. Air

service from Logan's present site is therefore restricted; increasing

demand will render these limitations even more detrimental in the future.

### 1.3    Seaport Problems

With the rise of successful trucking, rail, and air operations,

America's traditional shipping industry has declined. The superior

efficiency, and consequent lower total costs, of air and land transport

attracts many users, especially those who ship very valuable low-

volume goods. In response to this competition, two major technological

advances have been conceived for the shipping industry. Over-all ship

size has been increased. A tanker which holds 20 to 25 times more

cargo than was carried by ships during World War II can offer lower

shipping prices per unit. Second, containerization of general bulk cargo

can revolutionize cargo handling procedures, reducing time in port,

cargo waiting time, and making theft virtually obsolete (Figure 1.2).

Increased reliability and speedier shipping would inspire users to

return to shipping service.

Of course, new technologies must be adopted and must be

attended by appropriate alterations in over-all operations, if they are

to work, and herein lies the wide discrepancy in current East Coast

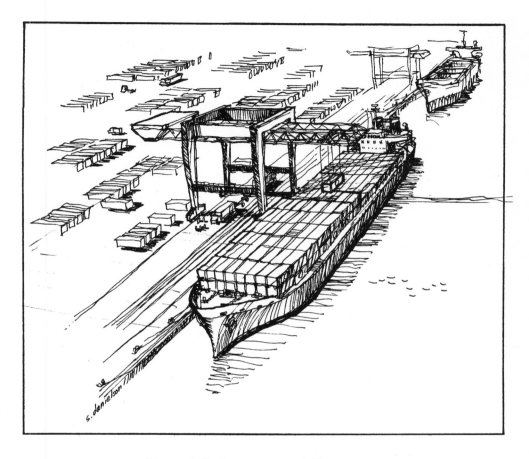

Figure 1.2 Containerized Shipping

port success. Boston has not built the facilities, has not bought the equip-

ment, has not achieved the procedures needed for successful containerized

shipping. The city has failed to construct suitable marshalling areas and

access routes to city storage centers and regional highways. Wide shipping

lanes have not been created. Rather than these physical prerequisites to

modern shipping, Boston continues to offer the small sheltered inlets, the

uncooperative labor attitudes, the primitive docks, warehouses, and cargo handling of traditional shipping.

The first to suffer would be the shipper, for obsolete methods mean higher costs. But for many shippers the solution is simple: ship from a better port. For remaining users, resulting cargo delays spiral costs higher. Service to Boston must be further reduced. The dying port of Boston is its own victim.

One can largely attribute regressive policy to relations between Boston's labor and management. Unions refuse to permit modern procedures, yet, on the other hand, management does not press to modernize or to establish a viable compromise.

The port is also handicapped by its present location. Space is lacking for the installation of needed equipment. The Harbor is located in the oldest part of the city; narrow streets cannot adequately serve truck traffic (even major highways, notably the Southeast Expressway, cannot accommodate car and truck traffic emanating from the Harbor.) Active facilities are interspersed among rotting docks (Figure 1.3), further inhibiting port efficiency.

Figure 1.3 Rotting Docks

For a city so pressed for housing and open recreational areas, so mindful of the beauty and natural value of the ocean, the disintegrating port is not alone a "seaport problem". Unprofitable and unsound docks preclude other urban uses. Shipping, though fitful, pollutes the harbor's waters. The problem of the Port of Boston is the problem of the city of Boston.

## 1.4   The Airport and Seaport Viewed Together

Logic dictates the parallel study of subsystems performing similar functions within a total transportation system. Consequently, the Boston airport and seaport situations were compared. Both ports occupy sites in the city harbor, both provide the region with terminals for cargo and passenger service, neither is sufficiently accessible for much of the metropolitan area. The airport lacks room to expand; the seaport withers from insufficient demand.

Such simple observations as well as more intricate relationships suggested solutions - why not give seaport lands to the airport? - which in turn transmuted into real innovative proposals - why not move airport functions to distant harbor islands, give airport land to consolidated seaport functions, thus freeing harbor land for other urban development? A unified concern for both ports contributed essentially to the final Project BOSPORUS design.

## 1.5   The Design Overview

Project BOSPORUS represents an attempt to comprehend the problems of Boston as a port and to create a design whose implementation would eliminate or minimize present and future transport troubles. By

examining the port in its several contexts, as a functioning node of the

transportation system of the region and country, as a physical portion

of the metropolitan community, and as a social and economic influence

on the region, one can determine, in general, port characteristics and

criteria, and the costs of solving port problems. A summary of the

resulting design forms the remainder of this chapter. A detailed account

of decision-making, precise recommendations, and the design will

follow in succeeding chapters of this book.

Our airport design responds primarily to trends in the aircraft

industry and in Boston's air traffic. We believe that large, fast,

fixed-wing jetcraft will dominate long-haul flight service. Social

pressure, discontent with noise and pollution, will dictate removal

of fixed-wing airports from population centers. V/STOL[3], on the other

hand, appears virtually free of social annoyances. We therefore think

that V/STOL will assume the numerous short distance, "shuttle" flights

to New York, Philadelphia, Washington, and other smaller cities formerly

assigned to CTOL[4] flights. V/STOL will operate from small ports close

to or in the midst of urban activity centers. Air traffic control techniques

and instrumentation are expected to improve to the point that V/STOL

and fixed-wing operations may proceed simultaneously in close proximity.

---

[3] Vertical/Short Take-Off and Landing
[4] Conventional Take-Off and Landing

Figure 1.4 depicts our total port design. We recommend the removal of all long-range jet service from Logan Airport to a proposed new runway area in and around the Brewster Islands in the Outer Harbor. These facilities would include runways, taxiways, operations for minimal aircraft servicing, and special aircraft loading platforms (Figure 1.5). Projections stating that Logan runways will be saturated by 1975 justify the construction of a second runway system. The location fulfilled social and economic criteria; of a number of possible airport sites, Brewster was found least expensive, yet maximally beneficial for the metropolitan region. Modified Logan terminals will offer primary staging functions not assigned to Brewster, thus preserving capital invested in Logan.

Typically, a jetliner will land at Brewster, taxi to a loading pad, and off-load its passengers and their luggage onto "mobile lounges". The lounges will then travel to Logan for passenger debarkation. Meanwhile, at Brewster, the airplane will be cleaned, reprovisioned, and then a new complement of passengers brought from Logan by the mobile lounge will board. The airplane will taxi to an outbound runway and take off. Only landing, take-off, aircraft turn-around procedures, servicing, and baggage transfer will occur at Brewster.

The mobile lounges will drive at high speeds over a special roadway, eventually to be adapted to a fully automated guideway system, to the major passenger terminal located at the present Logan site. (An extension of this roadway might link the South Shore to Logan; consideration

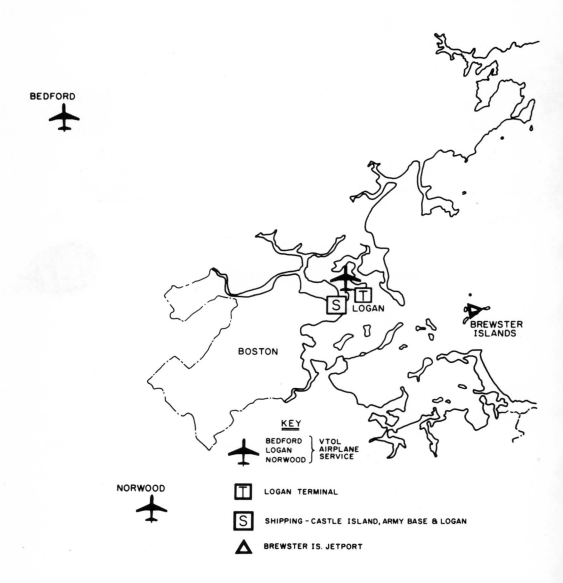

Figure 1.4 BOSPORUS Seaport and Airport Design

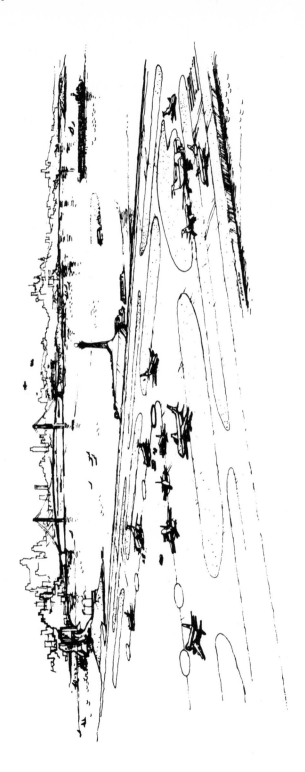

Figure 1.5 Brewster Jetport

should also be given to using such a route to provide rapid access to the

North Shore.) At Logan, passenger luggage will be delivered and retrieved,

tickets will be processed, small shops and colateral services such as

car rental and hotel reservation booths will reside. A rational layout of

all services will minimize passenger walking. Automated baggage-handling

and ticketing systems will speed travelers through the terminal.

One of three V/STOL sites planned for the Boston region will also

operate at Logan. The remaining two ports will be built at Hanscom Field

in Bedford and Norwood Airport in Norwood, both of which are convenient

to Route 128. V/STOL aircraft will handle all short-haul flights. Physical

and time connections between V/STOL and long-range flights at Logan will

be optimized. General aviation will be permitted at all three ports. Of

Boston's present traffic, 70% consists of short-haul flights. Logan's share

of future Boston service may thus be reduced by as much as 75%[5].

This plan will provide facilities for all types of users while cur-

tailing undesirable and inefficient aspects of air service. One of the three

short flight facilities will be within convenient distance, thus reducing

airport access times. "Local" direct service to New York, Philadelphia,

and Washington city centers will save users trip time. V/STOL craft

produce far less noise and pollution. Noisy jets will be banished to the

Outer Harbor.

Perhaps the above system contributes most significantly to over-all

---

5      $\dfrac{70}{3} = 23$

      $100 - 23 = 77$

port efficiency by reforming Logan land use. Large runways will be

replaced partially by expanded terminal and cargo operations, and a

V/STOL port. Excess land may be developed as an automated seaport

terminal, storage, transfer, and marshalling areas. The remaining

tracts may be sold to industry or used for recreation.

    The most dramatic portion of our design may be a development

proposal to rejuvenate Boston's seaport. While we anticipate that

the port will, in fact, revive, we have provided for the port's historic-

ally tangled and unpredictable affairs by including in our plan numerous

evaluation and decision points. Even a more settled port would demand

such an adaptive plan given the constant changes in the cargo transport

industry. Boston can decide its future role in the nation's seaborne

transportation with the aid of a plan that spells out the repercussions

of each alternative major decision.

    In addition, at a minimal cost the city may adopt independent

portions of our proposal that remain valid regardless of the direction of

general port evolution. We suggest that storage areas for petroleum

and other liquid bulk cargoes be linked by pipeline to the Outer Harbor.

Tank farms on the lower end of Chelsea Creek should be moved to vacant

land in the upper Creek area, unifying these storage facilities. Supertankers

can then call on the Port of Boston without entering the traditional harbor.

Oil need no longer spill and pollute during transfer operations. Consoli-

dation of port facilities can begin at once, independent of any further

development plan. Large sections of the Inner Harbor would thus be freed

for other urban development and a general clean-up of Boston Harbor shores
and waters could begin.

Solution of the labor problem must precede any seaport development.
Labor must willingly agree to operate new or renovated facilities. The
Boston waterfront has had a long history of labor difficulties, many of
which stem from union efforts to maintain outmoded practices out of a fear
of losing wages. Labor conservatism takes the form of overly restrictive
work rules and general resistance to technological innovation. Fortunately,
the situation is far from hopeless. Patterns of labor-management cooperation
have begun to develop, particularly for grievance procedures. The union
leaders, although flamboyant in public, sincerely care about the welfare
of their following. Labor's dawning realization that a dead port provides
no jobs is a final source of hope.

Acceptance of modernized procedures and equipment may be speeded
by an offer of short term labor benefits. The natural attrition rate for
longshoremen can be accelerated by lowering the retirement age to 62 and
raising pensions. An option for retired men to work up to eight hours a
week until they reach 67 promotes a sense of independence, as well as
providing extra income.

After a labor and management accord, the first step toward reju-
venation, consolidation of facilities, can be undertaken. As a beginning,
the presently existing container facility at Castle Island would be opened.
By 1974, the remainder of port operations would be handled by facilities
to be constructed at the Army Base. These two areas would shoulder the

burden of port operation until the conversion of Logan. With jetcraft

relocation, construction could begin of a third seaport facility at

Logan which would be so situated that a ship need traverse the basin

in one direction only. Shipping activities at Logan will in no way

interfere with the V/STOL and airport terminal which will have replaced

the Logan CTOL port. Facilities will accommodate the most modern

cargo handling techniques. At any one time, the harbor will be able

to berth 20 ships.

Such massive development can take place only if shippers

respond to lower costs made possible by the use of automated cargo

handling techniques. Shipping to and from modern Castle Island

should start the trend toward lower costs. As automated facilities

grow, progressively lower costs will attract trade which will use the

new areas at full potential. Today's vicious circle of inefficiency-

greater costs-reduced business reverses to become a spiraling of

efficiency-lower costs-growing demand.

The management of this future port operation must differ vastly

from that presently in command. The current administration lacks

managerial initiative; government transportation agencies fail to

coordinate their efforts; port policy does not respond to issues of

public welfare. Given the advanced technologies which shall operate,

these deficiencies may best be alleviated by a centralized administration

of all state transport activities. We therefore propose the creation of a

Massachusetts Department of Transportation to combine all relevant state supported agencies into one administration. It will also offer aid

solicited by independent local bodies. The primary mission of the M.D.T.

will be to create a master plan for all transportation systems within

the state, and to annually update this plan in accordance with the quality

of past performance and with revised technological, social and economic

predictions.

     To directly administer Boston's ports, we propose a Metropolitan

Port Commission, possessing powers at the same level and of the same

scope as the D.P.W., M.D.C., M.B.T.A., and a private development corpor-

ation, PORTAD. The M.P.C. will determine policy for the port and will own all

port land and some port facilities which it will lease to PORTAD. The M.P.C.

and PORTAD will subsequently interrelate as follows: the M.P.C. can under-

write some of the cost of port capitalization; it will dictate port policy

(in accordance with the M.D.T. transportation plan). Through ownership

of land and facilities, as leaser, it will be able to control PORTAD.

PORTAD will raise the remaining capital and will operate the port so as to

earn substantial profits for private investors. Incentive is thereby provided

to operate efficiently, imaginatively, and progressively, within the policies

established by the M.P.C. By dividing the policy and the operational control

of the port, we aim to minimize the risk of loss to the general public and

to maximize gain for the entrepreneurs. Figure 1.6 is a diagram of port

management and finance relations.

     Our plan outlines improvements solely in the two major terminal

systems, yet it implies a challenge to Boston city planners and developers.

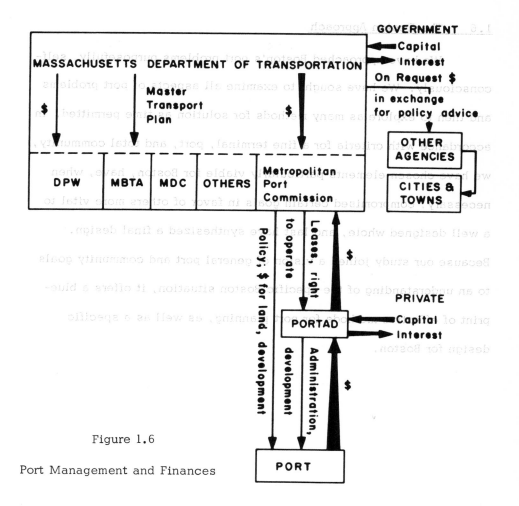

Figure 1.6

Port Management and Finances

As planned, the consolidated transportation facilities will occupy locations
convenient to users yet which least deprive the community of valuable land.
In some cases, large tracts, currently unused, would be freed.  The
relocation of jetcraft and certain seaport operations would reduce air and
water pollution.  Upon these reclaimed physical resources, others may
exercise their imaginative concern for Boston.

1.6     The Design Approach

We have approached Boston's port problems purposefully, self-consciously. We have sought to examine all aspects of port problems and then to explore as many methods for solution as time permitted. In accordance with criteria for a fine terminal, port, and total community, we have chosen elements particularly viable for Boston, have, when necessary, compromised certain goals in favor of others more vital to a well designed whole, and last have synthesized a final design. Because our study joined a vision of general port and community goals to an understanding of the specific Boston situation, it offers a blue-print of effective methods for port planning, as well as a specific design for Boston.

Chapter $2$

DESIGN CRITERIA

The intent of this chapter is to place the engineering design of the
port in its proper perspective: to examine the relevance of our project to
clearly identified social objectives and other essential, and at times conflicting needs which any major transportation development must heed. Both
the economic and the social viewpoint toward such a design are investigated
in order to develop for each its own criteria for acceptability. This concern
for the larger significance of a transportation system does not postdate our
design in an attempt to justify final conclusions; it was part of the procedure
which produced this design.

This chapter ideally resembles the conscience of the designer, for
given a mandate to alter an organic environment, he must temper measures
which provide a far more efficient transportation network with a concern for
those who would be adversely affected by the realization of a technically
perfect blueprint. He must be attuned to the broader, long-range repercussions
of the design.

We could not evaluate in anything approaching its true complexity the social and economic life a design affects. Yet an honest outline of the

general goals of each, as we perceived them, enabled us to measure our

engineering plans against broader essentials. The strong illusion of our

design acting on familiar human patterns, and on people whose needs we

had acknowledged, helped to raise us from participants in an academic

exercise to the conscientious planners we came to see as the only possible

creators of a good design.

## 2.1    Economic Processes

Within the scope of our project, we could by no means examine the

complexity of our nation's economic processes; however, there are several

observations that have led to our final designs and decisions. First, in

a technically advanced and industrialized nation such as ours, there is a

need for continued revitalization and streamlining of the entire economic

workings from producer to consumer. Recent and continuing technical advance-

ments, primarily in the area of computer technology, have provided the means

and tools for modernized methods and facilities which can increase production

and make it more efficient. In addition to the actual computer aided tech-

niques for economic advancement, the computer has also provided evaluative

and decision-making capabilities to the economic community. (Thereby has

arisen a new process, systems analysis, which utilizes the computer's

analytical abilities.) One can program a computer to evaluate an entire

economic picture, a far cry from the tedious task of piecemeal analysis and

improvement of the components of a production system. Utilization of this technique has shown the standards which must be met by each link in a

system if the flow of goods is not to be constricted.

Transportation, of course, vitally supports our economic system.

Several obstacles, however, continue to block improvements and modifi-

cation of the transporation system. First, the sytem, at present, consists

of a wide variety of transportation modes, each made up of components of

varying degrees of efficiency and modernity. Confusion inevitably arises

from attempting to interface these modes. The gains in efficiency due to

containerization, the first step toward development of a network in which

goods flow smoothly, will be offset by the increased volume of cargo

projected for the future; only a modern countrywide transportation system

will be able to take full advantage of ingenious transport components pre-

sently being invented and introduced. (Our present system could be com-

pared to a garment factory where a machine capable of cutting out thousands

of garment pieces an hour provides these pieces to women sewing by hand.)

Transportation facilities, unlike production lines, cannot be altered

overnight. Unlike a new computer system or a new marketing technique,

these facilities will be available only after years of planning and contruction.

Countless political and economic hurdles must be cleared before permission

to build is obtained and before actual operation begins. Due to inadequate

foresight or lack of adequate funding the facilities may be overcrowded or

outmoded before the first day of use.

Moreover, transportation systems are extremely costly. For many

systems funding must be cleared through legislative action or referendum and bond issues. Furthermore, they may be accompanied by secondary

effects in the form of noise or obtrusive physical facilities whose adverse

social characteristics may affect numerous people not directly concerned

with the benefits from the new system. Additional social-political hurdles

must therefore be surmounted. Finally, transportation construction may be

of a scope which transforms immediate environments and permanently alters

entire regions. Little wonder that transportation proposals are being increasing-

ly scrutinized.

Yet to return to economic considerations, the price society now pays

to satisfy its transport needs points to the necessity for better transport

planning and improved facilities for our transportation system. The only

other systems of comparable magnitude, the mail and telephone systems,

are both showing signs of strangulation, the victims of cost constrictions

The most handicapped system, transportation, must be capable of functioning

in the overcrowded 1970's and beyond, yet must not become so monstrous

and complex as to become self-defeating. The facilities must be constructed;

there is no doubt of their need; but also a united effort must be made to

choose between alternatives, priorities, and systems themselves.

## 2.2    The Social Processes

Transportation systems can create social detriments which range

from immediate health hazards to regional destruction, from the displacement

of members of tight knit communities to the despoiling of natural resources.

Many more social than economic criteria for good design may therefore be listed, and many of these seek the protection of present conditions rather than the institution of positive changes. Yet the planner must look beyond the possible ills he may cause and not only prevent them, but also relieve situations that appear totally unconnected to transportation. Such an approach should be the final goal of the responsible planner, but first he must consider the three typical problem areas that have come to be falsely viewed as the inevitable accompaniment of new transportation networks.

The nationwide problems of pollution and noise are receiving much attention. Social pressure against toxic exhaust fumes and jet noise is sufficiently strong that reduction in these intrusions on our environment is becoming a national issue. Standards are being established as a basis for controlling the emission from gasoline engines and the noise and pollution from future aircraft. On the local level, the depollution of Boston harbor is receiving a growing base of support. In sum, those problems which are not Boston's alone are finding solutions thanks to both governmental and industrial efforts.

The displacement of communities, neighborhoods, and individuals for the purpose of building new highways or airports receives intensive debate each time it occurs, but massive, continuing resistance has not formed due to the piecemeal, local nature of these infringements. Even within one city it is difficult to maintain a group which would in each instance protest and thereby block such intrusions. As long as resistance is limited to those few directly threatened at any one time by a new transportation facility, failure will continue. The planner may confidently proceed, relatively sure of the weakness of his adversaries. Alternately, he may incorporate

in his plan either measures to preserve living patterns, or to provide new

social benefits which will tend to offset any harm he cannot avoid causing.

Last, the planner must consider a danger which he, most of all,

should realize and strive to prevent. Few others see it at present, and many

would be indifferent were they told of it. New construction methods allow

for little differentiation or uniqueness in designs. Architects are not trained

to be sensitive to enduring local patterns and forms, but learn to create

designs appropriate to specifications rather than specific locations. The

architectural traditions of cities, and of entire regions, are thereby threatened.

Citizens will suffer a loss in individuality as they no longer feel themselves

attached to a unique place. The diminution of local tradition would be felt

with particular keenness in New England. Transportation construction has

been especially guilty of neutralizing the areas in which it builds. One can

predict with considerable accuracy the area that will grow up around a new

airport: the miles of shopping center, acres of parking spaces, even the

names of the chains of support facilities and hamburg drive-ins, all identical

across the country. Terminals for other modes tend to be even more uniform

in appearance. Destruction of an entire region's heritage does not offend

the economic sector nor many of those sensitive to social problems. It is

primarily a spiritual loss. Nevertheless, it should be prevented.

Now let us return to the idea of the planner who would not only prevent

social misfortunes but also provide benefits beyond those stemming from

improved transport itself. A project such as ours would be realized within an area already replete with problems. Alterations in transportation facilities throughout the core of Boston are contemplated and currently in progress. Is it not possible to include in the final design recommendations, proposals, and designs which will simultaneously improve transportation and ease other urban ills? Certainly the secondary effects of a construction project may become an asset to the city rather than an annoyance or an outright problem.

The complexity of conflicting social needs must not drive the planner back to the simpler realms of economic gain and technical superiority. If these needs are complex, it is because they reflect the primary life that economics and technology serve.

## 2.3    Interdisciplinary Design Approach

In the preceding sections two conflicting viewpoints have been elaborated. On one hand a claim to economic need emerges, easily supported by statistics, and simply justified by an expected return greater than the cost of the investment. On the other hand, the costs, benefits, and disbenefits for relevant social issues are frequently omitted on the basis that they are indeterminant. The social issues are not presented in an organized fashion and often these issues are of such complexity that one cannot readily understand them. (A builder may pay relocation costs for a few families, but does this payment in any way make up for personal harm or for the sociological change in the neighborhood.) Such confrontations may involve merely semantic differences, but economic processes which cry for more consolidated, unified, and efficient systems may constitute a basic threat to the individual and his

immediate environment. Obviously one need not consider this an "either, or"
question, for in fact neither point of view necessarily excludes the other,
and neither is predominantly right.

What path then leads to reasonable design? How can separate viewpoints contribute fairly to the solution? Given a reasonably clear economic
analysis, how may blurred social factors be incorporated into the final plan?

The Project BOSPORUS approach has been to present every reasonable
alternative, and to determine the one which will most nearly satisfy the
specific situation. This sort of broad base investigation is called the interdisciplinary approach because the design team consists of representatives
of each discipline concerned with such a project. The "planner" is then
the corporate being formed of those interested in the project. Vocal members
insure that no issue or alternative will be missed because of oversight.
Decisions represent compromises and compensations hammered out among
all members. Compromise may vary from proposing symbolic consideration
for the dissenting discipline or group to abandoning really objectionable ideas.
The final design in any specific case may not be predicted.

## 2.4     The Criteria of Design

In an attempt to find a key to a successful large scale undertaking,
a series of interrelated criteria were developed which show both a progression
toward a decision and in retrospect appear to have been the guidelines of
our project. In the optimum situation, the venture would be economically
necessary, would represent a sound financial investment, and would be

efficient, incorporating all technological advances into the design. At the same time, social effects of such a project would all be positive, no adverse affects would be visited on either the environment or citizens, and the community would be substantially strengthened. Then obviously all possible criteria would be met. The preceding is quite clearly an ideal. If these criteria cannot be met, then the interdisciplinary approach reverts to the more realistic sphere of alternatives and compromises. To produce valuable compromises, consistent in their intent, an ordering of priorities had to be established. It consisted of the following:

1) The project must spring from widespread need; it must reflect the desires of a large segment of the population. It would also be desirable if such a need was felt by the physical neighbors of transportation facilities.

2) Its service must be relevant to people as individuals, both to the shipper a thousand miles away and the citizen whose back yard it passes.

3) It should promote positive social interaction and be a source of pride to the community.

4) It should be directed not solely at the problems for which it was originally intended, but also at the problems of its immediate surroundings.

5) If some citizens fall victim to severely adverse affects, they must be compensated. This may involve possible recompense spelled out in the design. In the eyes of those affected, a fair

repayment must be achieved.

6) There must be preservation of the natural resources of air, water, and land, and the possibility of additional use of these resources for the community.

7) The impact of the design upon the city during construction must be fully explained and made as innocuous as possible.

If one follows guidelines such as these a fine, necessary facility can be built with public support rather than against protest. Not only efficient systems but a stronger community will be forged. In comparing alternatives, the one that brings the most benefits at the least cost, financial and social, must be the basis of the final plan.

## 2.5    BOSPORUS

In creating Project BOSPORUS, we did, in fact, follow these design criteria as closely as possible. Let us cite some of the most dramatic instances of our response to these criteria. Our choice of a location for a major jetport was based second on cost and engineering feasibility, first on the possibility of alleviating the noise problems of the North Shore without afflicting another populated region. Several Harbor islands would be used, but the outer islands were chosen since air traffic there would not preclude the use of the rest of the Harbor space for recreation or other purposes. The retention of the Logan terminals maintains financial benefits and employment opportunities enjoyed by the North Shore communities which have been so closely tied to the airport. The airport location remains convenient to the

Boston core industrial region, one of Logan's assets we wished to retain in a modern jetport. An airport in the Outer Harbor represents a physical symbol of the vitality of the city of Boston. It represents an engineering achievement to be proud of, an economic asset, and, unlike nearly all other major airports, does not create social evils.

The fruits of applying our interdisciplinary method to the seaport are also evident. Elimination of immediate social and economic ills was called for in the first phase of development. An end to the oil and pollution problem within the Inner Harbor took first priority along with consolidation of existing shipping facilities. Subsequent development was left to future decision makers. Revitalization of a greater Boston seaport facility was offered as a viable possibility, with site specifications and recommendations offered. This second phase of seaport development is inherently tied to both the airport designs and land use possibilities. With the relocation of the jetport, enormous amounts of land at Logan are freed for alternate use. If sufficient demand for an expanded seaport arises, the land would be available. If this is not the case, the land may be utilized by the city as a whole in other ways. Our key contribution in this instance was providing means for solving future problems by creative solution to an existing problem. The Logan land and other acreage in the inner harbor region could well become housing centers, the basis for expanded recreation facilities, or both. The contribution of this freed land would be nullified, however, if it were developed in a piecemeal fashion rather than as part of a persistent campaign against the severe problems affecting Boston.

While we concentrated particularly on the problems of the inner city, our recommendations also aid the suburban dweller with his transportation problems. Multiple locations for the commuter V/STOL ports return him virtually to his doorway. This convenience may be enjoyed for reasonable economic costs and without excessive noise. Terminals in suburban locations provide the secondary benefits of reduced travel, therefore reduces crowding, on city arteries.

So the BOSPORUS proposals do not merely display engineering competency; rather they reflect a thinking process, a series of commitments and compromises, all undertaken with the goal of making Boston a better city by improving the air and sea terminal facilities. Many of the final decisions were left open, not because we lacked the inclination to choose, but because, consistent with our philosophy, the constituants, the parties actually concerned with the future of sea transportation in this city, or pollution, or noise, should in actuality be the decision makers for a project of this magnitude. Our goal was to provide the means by which Boston might solve many of its urban problems simultaneously, by focusing on a limited number of developments which, taken together, have the potential for relieving many problems.

Chapter 3

SITE SELECTION: PROBLEMS

3.1    Approaches to the Problem

In dealing with the problem of terminal site selection, we have

particularly sought to achieve a comprehensive approach, comprehensive

in the sense that all relevant aspects of the problem at hand are weighed

and valued conscientiously (Figure 3.1). Our object has been to enter

into the design process with entirely open minds, to advance at the pace

needed to grasp all the implications of a design, and to study all potential

problem sources so that they will never become troublesome through neglect

or oversight. Past planning had tended to be characterized by oversimplified

vision and the admittance of only that evidence tending to confirm a plan

favored a priori. Yet only objective research seems reasonable in an area

such as site selection in which one encounters the nebulous, unfathomed

problems of urban technology and environment.

The comprehensive approach, then, implies discriminating evaluation

of past procedures and the introduction of appropriate change in methods.

To assure this, engineering should couple, during the design and planning

33

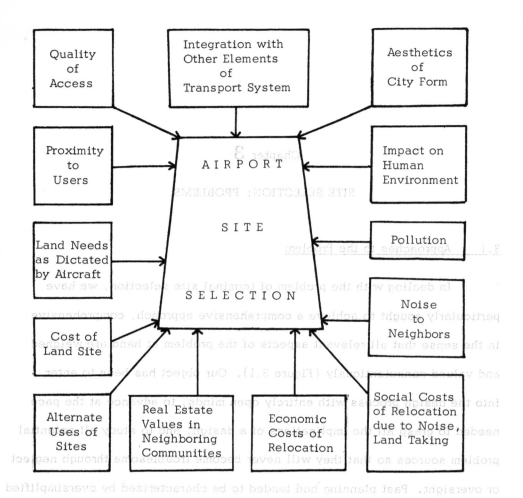

Figure 3.1 Elements Determining Airport Site Selection

stage, with the social sciences, a union apt to insure examination of the

whole range of significant issues which must be appraised before decision.

However technologically and economically feasible, a project should

qualify for development only if social disruption would be minimal. In the

final design, improved transport facilities must equally promote positive social gain and financial growth.

Our preoccupation with the route to this design goal stems, not
from narcissism, but from the conviction that the comprehensive, systems
approach should be developed as a tool available for numerous independent
problems. Our task is twofold: to design specific sea and air terminals,
and to create a generalized decision making procedure. The plan for
Boston can be thought to spring from the application of a far more essential
methodology (though in our designing, the chicken and egg assist one
another).

3.2    Implicit Attitude and Explicit Philosophy

Among the complexes indispensable to sustaining urban life, the
transportation system emerges as the most difficult to analyze and upgrade.
The major reason, briefly, is that while transportation acts as a sine qua
non of economic and technological progress, the physical presence of
transportation facilities, whether pathways or terminals, proves communally
detrimental. Whereas an office building offers its community employment,
not to mention a taxable structure, an asphalt swath across countryside
or neighborhoods comforts no one. A new industry may displace families,
but the revenue added to the community usually affords far more consolation
than exhaust fumes and noise, the chief local by-products of a transportation
network.

Furthermore, transport is only the means to an end. In that sense,
transportation and its returns appear more abstract than other systems.

Although the general public readily finds fault with its attributes, especially

if they function poorly, rarely do individuals or communities see the need

for voluntary sacrifice for the sake of transportation.

The economic and industrial segment of the community today presses

for increasingly fast and efficient transportation systems at the expense

of the residential sector. This appears just - the industrial population is

also the residential population - only if one ignores the key parameter

of social stratification. The working majority, living in older, more unified

communities, has been the primary group to suffer from the construction and

implementation of new transportation systems, while higher income users

have reaped the benefits of more efficient transport. To oversimplify, this

means that the blue collar worker must move so his white collar boss can

fly from a more convenient airport.

The implicit assumption of many past projects has been that one may

rightfully sacrifice well established lower class community life to the

convenience and economic gain of the middle and upper classes. In place

of this tacit attitude, we propose the comprehensive approach, not only as

the best path to an intelligent design, but also as an explicit philosophy of

concern for all.

### 3.3    Terminal Defined

What is the purpose of transportation terminals; what impact, what

importance, and what primary characteristics do they possess? These

questions answered, a decision making process may be developed.

From a functional viewpoint, the terminal is a node in the transportation system, perhaps the most vital part because users characterize
the modes of transport by their terminals, the points of departure and
arrival, the visible monuments to transportation activity. At these
embarkation-debarkation points occur accumulation and sorting of cargo
and people, fare collection, vehicle maintenance and storage. Collaterally
the terminal offers insurance, food and gift concessions, and personal
services. This spectrum of internal operation proceeds regardless of the
terminal's location. As long as the terminal lies convenient to established
modes of transportation, and sufficiently close to the city's supply areas,
other factors in terminal site selection (from the point of view of transport
only) appear marginal.

To seize upon other relevant aspects, air and sea terminals may
be viewed as interfaces; between geographic features; between modes of
transport; and between the community of users and the transport network.
It can be imagined as a knot which ties together the various threads of
the total transport system. And as a knot impedes the progress of a
"rope walker", the present terminal activities characteristically slow the
progress of a trip. Or again, the transportation system can be visualized
literally as a network overlaying the quilt of city neighborhoods, cutting
through a variety of social functions. When people lose more by its
presence than they gain by its services, problems arise.

The ideal solution can also be represented metaphorically.
Consider the terminal as a valve, regulating the flow in the total trans-

portation system. From the engineering and technical vantage, wide

latitude may exist in selecting location, but the valve must be constructed

to function as efficiently as possible. From a social viewpoint, the

valve's situation is the most critical issue. If an internally efficient

terminal can be placed at a convenient point where a minimum number of

people will feel adverse effects, all will agree that the purposes and

characteristics of a terminal will have been achieved.

### 3.4    Problem Statement and Methodology Outline

In dealing with transportation terminals in the Boston area, we
are confronted by two problems whose solutions conflict at several points.
On one hand, demand continues for expanded air services, both in Boston
and in the nation. Yet on the other, present use already places severe
burdens on the only large airport in the region, Logan International Airport.
It is estimated that 1975 will see its runways and terminal facilities
filled beyond capacity. Because the planning and construction of large
projects requires time, one must now consider the alternatives which might
best accommodate the needed additional service.

The present airport, lying close to the city and to vital transfer
points, enjoys a favorable location in terms of the transportation system
itself; however as a neighbor it grows daily more objectionable to
surrounding communities. Frequent innundations of high noise levels
have provoked loud verbal objection to present operation and especially
to plans for increased operation and expanded facilities.

To achieve a solution acceptable to user needs and community

demands three factors were, of necessity, considered: the economics of

present operation and future alternatives, possible technological improve-

ment, and the social implications of each alternative. The preponderance

of this chapter deals with these issues.

As for the Port of Boston, only limited social problems have been

associated with its operations; rather, the difficulty has been economic.

Therefore, in regard to the possible future course of a seaport in Boston,

the major tradeoffs occur between technological advances and economics,

with the social well-being of the city and region as a measure of the

effectiveness of each alternative.

3.5     Relocation

The extent of the relocation which must accompany any new port

development is an important criterion of the potential of a particular port

site. By "relocation" we mean the physical displacement of dwelling

units and residents in order that adequate port facilities may be constructed.

In the case of an airport for jumbo-jets and/or SST craft, the problem of

relocation divides into:

1) displacement for the purposes of port construction, and

2) displacement caused by intolerable noise levels.

The first category of displacement involves complete removal of existing

facilities; the second is more selective.

The extent of objection to and the costs of relocation depend strongly upon one crucial decision: will relocated families be given fair

remuneration for their property and then be aided in finding alternate

housing on the open market, or will the relocators construct housing

for them? The chosen path will deeply influence the price of relocation

and may have some bearing on associated problems. Where a very large

number of families are to be relocated (say, upwards of 5,000 people)

and the time given for such relocation is relatively small (say under one

year), it may well be impossible to find the necessary amount, or type,

of housing on the open market. This situation would limit the choice by

dictating new construction, the more costly alternative.

One must also consider human factors which tend to make relocation

more or less of a problem. In the first place, the extent of the problem

of relocating families is not a linear function of the number of families

moved. The difficulties increase at a greater rate than the number of

families, chiefly because a large, cohesive group possesses greater

associated political power and can marshal more hostility to moving.

Another influential aspect is the social class and ethnic background

of the population to be relocated. The more socially and ethnically homo-

geneous the community, the more resistance it will offer to such

relocation. Lower middle class urban dwellers resist change more than

upper middle class suburbanites. Although the former group lacks the

political power of the suburbanites, they do feel a sincere attachment to

their neighborhood and a willingness to fight for it.

Relocation disrupts the life processes of people and this, too, must be reckoned in a full evaluation of the problem. For example, how does relocation affect access to work? A move from one community to another might not alter access for suburbanites who work in the city; on the other hand, a more centrally located community, especially a poorer one where residents may not own automobiles, may be seriously incapacitated by such a movement. Furthermore, relocation may annoy those people who are accustomed to moving from place to place, but tight-knit social units, some members of which have spent their entire lives in a small geographic area, might find relocation traumatic[1].

One may estimate the cost of relocation by counting the number of families to be moved and multiplying that figure by the average remuneration for property, or one could estimate the cost of building adequate housing for the number of relocated families. Depending upon the relevance of the preceding factors, one or the other of these approaches will be preferable. In no case, however, should one assume that this figure fully represents the costs of moving. It is simply a first approximation, and must be taken as such.

Yet no matter what the solution, relocation is at heart unjust in that the costs and benefits with which one must deal do not apply to the same individuals. While the community at large benefits from an expanded

---

[1] An account of this problem, termed the "grief factor", may be found in Urban Renewal edited by James Wilson. M.I.T. Press, Cambridge, Massachusetts, 1966.

airport, some subsection of that community suffers the costs. The problem

becomes particularly acute when the burden falls upon those who least

frequently benefit as individuals from the new facility. This inequality may

give pause but cannot be permitted to impede progress since such difficulties

attend almost every public works project. Yet one must not ignore the problem.

If people must be relocated, the obligation falls to society to provide for

them adequate and decent housing and to alleviate some of the discomforts

of displacement.

## 3.6    Real Estate Values

Airports diminish the residential desirabilit of land by introducing

two by-products: noise and pollution. Very few people want to live in

an area of high noise levels. On the other hand, many people hope to

live within easy access of airport facilities. How then does the presence

of an airport affect real estate values? This question may be a criterion

in evaluating possible sites although, admittedly, it is not a leading

consideration. Yet given two otherwise equal locations, land value rather

than chance should determine one's choice. If real estate values are

influenced by airports, this fact should enter into the decision making

process.

Unfortunately, information sufficient to answer these questions

unequivocally and in general form is lacking. The one study of this

particular problem yielded conclusions that one may certainly contest.

While looking for a site for a fourth airport, the New York Port

Authority commissioned H.O. Walther of Chicago to explore real estate
values in the general vicinity of airports in the United States. [2] Walther
chose five airports:

   1) Kennedy Airport, New York

   2) O'Hare Airport, Chicago

   3) San Francisco International Airport, San Francisco

   4) United States Naval Air Station, Glenview, Illinois

   5) United States Naval Air Station, Moffett Field, California

He selected strips of real estate near the airports (in all directions) and
areas at some distance. He considered only those pieces sold twice
during a ten year period. Based on a total of 400 transactions, he
concluded that airports have no effect on real estate values. More
specifically, he claimed that:

   1) There were no differences in the market values of land near
      the airports and the market value of land some distance away.

   2) There were no significant differences between the market
      value of land on the flight path and in other directions.

   3) No more houses were offered for sale in airport areas than
      in other locations.

   If indeed Walther formed correct conclusions, real estate values
are no problem and may be forgotten. Yet the validity of his conclusions

_____

[2] Walther, H.O., A Study of the Impact of Airports on the Market Value
of Real Estate in Adjacent Areas, H.O. Walther, Chicago, 1960.

are open to doubt for several reasons. Only if the sample of five airports

were randomly selected would generalization of the findings be proper.

Though Walther may indeed have selected randomly, his client's eagerness

to prove a case may also have swayed him toward a biased selection.

Similarly, Walther chose to look at those pieces of property sold

twice during a short period of time. This group, too, is not necessarily

a random sample. Twice-sold property may well boast equal market values

while other properties in the two areas differ significantly in value.

The date of the study, however, suggests a more important objection.

Published in 1960, the completed analysis preceded the advent of the jet

age. Since the noise problem has certainly intensified in the past few years,

Walther's results may well be outdated.

Ill-informed and unable to offer any general conclusion on the problem,

we nevertheless would like to state some observations which may be of use.

It is probably true that the effect of an airport on real estate values is

a function of the elasticity of land in that particular area. If it is at a

premium, for whatever reason, the presence of an airport will probably

not alter its worth. On the other hand, if people have a greater choice of

property, values will probably be undermined by airports.

Some indirect evidence appears that real estate values in East

Boston have been climbing in recent years. If true, it is clearly not

due to the attractiveness of the homes nor to the proximity of the airport.

A great number of the homes in the area appear less than perfect (average

value of owner-occupied homes in East Boston in 1960 was about $8,000) and the residents frequently complain about their monolithic next door

neighbor. But the East Boston (Figure 3.2) neighborhood apparently

has its attractions. Residents want to live amongst family and friends

in a tight-knit ethnic community. This was true in the West End before

renewal[3] and in the North End in the 1940's[4]. Land values remain at a

premium despite, not because of the airport.

In the case of Kennedy Airport in New York (assuming that Walther's

pre-jet-age results continue to be valid), one could argue that land in the

New York area also sells at a premium through supply and demand, and that

little or no elasticity exists there. On the other hand, situating an airport

in a sparsely populated suburban area where land abounds may downgrade

the land values by driving residents to other havens of suburban quiet

and content. Thus, an airport in or around Harvard, Massachusetts may

seriously devalue local real estate.

## 3.7    Cost of Land

Land cost ordinarily does not contribute greatly to the over-all

costs of construction. Yet the price will vary from site to site and, under

certain conditions, might certainly become prohibitive.

Land for public works can be purchased on the open market, but

customarily, eminent domain is required to keep the price at a reasonable

---

[3] Wilson, James, ed., Urban Renewal, The M.I.T. Press, Cambridge, 1966.
[4] Firey, Walter Irving, Land Use in Central Boston, The Harvard Press, Cambridge, 1947.

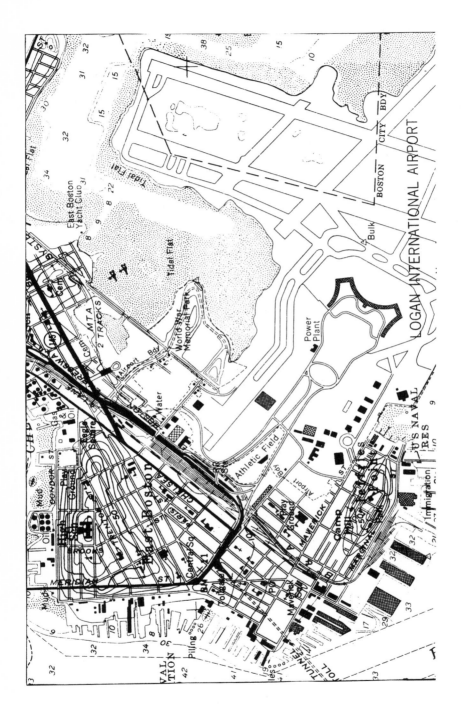

Figure 3.2 East Boston

level. In Massachusetts, the Port Authority cannot now exercise eminent

domain; the Legislative must grant special rights for every parcel of land

the Port Authority desires. Individual citizens can thereby obstruct M.P.A.

projects by exerting their political influence.

Eminent domain, when granted, provides only that the Authority

pay a fair price for the land. However, land costs comprehend more than

the simple cost of acreage in Eastern Massachusetts. They also include

the cost of businesses, industry, hotels, churches, schools, libraries,

etc. (We have included only residences under relocation costs.) As long

as one desires sparsely populated rural land, land costs remain reasonable,

but once one considers urbanized areas or even small towns, the costs

may skyrocket.

On the other hand, negative land costs can become an important

factor in the decision making process. By this we mean that the system

can benefit from the sale of unneeded sections of publicly owned land.

In the case of Boston particularly, the construction of airport facilities

in some location other than Logan would enable the Authority to divest

itself of much land now under its jurisdiction. Even if Logan were to be

retained as a V/STOL airport, a small fraction of the present land would

serve. If Logan is additionally retained as the most convenient central

passenger handling terminal, a larger piece of land would be utilized, but,

nevertheless, a great deal of land now occupied would be freed.

One could use land released in this manner in several ways.

Developers or industry could buy it and construct residential areas or attractive plants upon it.  Either eventuality would provide two financial

benefits:

    1)  Immediate revenues resulting from the sale of land would

        finance or repay construction of new facilities.

    2)  More land added to the city's tax rolls would increase the

        annual revenues.

Alternately, freed land could be the site of public works projects: parks,

libraries, city hospitals, etc.  While this move would not bring in increased

revenue, a complete analysis must include such alternatives since,

presumably, the city will be obliged to furnish such facilities in the

future somewhere within its boundaries.

    Both positive and negative land costs must be examined in the

evaluation scheme.  Positive land costs are, basically, a function of the

degree to which the land is developed.  Rural regions in Eastern Massa-

chusetts (not areas in which home construction or other such land use

is imminent) command on the order of $500 an acre.  Nascent residential

development would be accounted for under relocation rather than under

land costs.  However, intense land use adds enormous costs to the system

and these are reflected in non-linear land values.  Extensive urbanization,

or even suburbanization, is accompanied by a large number of retail stores,

gasoline stations, churches, restaurants, hotels, etc.  Thus, even though

the land area required may be less, the cost of utilizing the land can

increase very rapidly.

    Although negative land costs appear, at first glance, to be a

linear function of the value of the land (or, in other words, of the location),
one might correctly surmise a more complex relationship. Since Boston land
values are high, one would reap considerable revenue from the sale of
parts of Logan. However, if one offers a superabundance of land for sale
at one time (or during a relatively short period), the value of this land will
tend to decrease through simple supply and demand. Although land values
at times remain insensitive to demand, the M.P.A. would probably receive
a smaller profit by selling large chunks of land to developers than by
selling small parcels of land to prospective home owners to build independently. The plot of value vs. amount of land is, in any event, probably
non-linear and analysts must hold this in mind.

## 3.8     Characteristic Land Needs

Communities and social structures feel the presence of air facilities
in three ways. First, the terminal requires a particular parcel of land
taken from the region. Second, the area experiences by-products for some
distance from the port such as serious degrees of noise and pollution.
Similarly, traffic generated by the terminal pours onto the highways and
roads of neighboring regions. Third, in the immediate vicinity operations
directly essential to the airport's existence must be provided. One must
establish rights of way, zoning, police and regulatory assistance, and
city and regional access. Problems associated with this third, avowed
group of requirements appear minor indeed compared to those linked with
noise, pollution, and land absorption.

The aircraft themselves impose most of the terminal land require-

ments. An airport that hopes to operate under most prevailing wind

conditions requires at least two runway directions each of which must

be at least 10,000 feet long. Already this means four square miles of

land. When one adds all other needs, this figure rises to a limit of

approximately 15 square miles. Therefore a new airport's first requisite

is a land area of between 5 and 15 square miles, depending on the range

and use of the airport. The aircraft dictate, as well, that the airport,

at least the approaches to the runways and the runways themselves, be

situated in a relatively flat area. For maximum utilization, the airport

must be close, in time, to the major population and commercial centers

of the city. The ideal tract of land, then, would be large, flat and near

to the city center.

### 3.9    Peripheral Qualifications for Terminal Location

Sites which fulfill the basic land requirements stated above must

in turn satisfy a second category of qualifications which centers primarily

around the anathema of noise and pollution. The noise from modern jet-

craft extends nearly ten miles on either side of the approach path and

reaches a crescendo of intolerability at the airport. A study of severity

of disturbance versus social function and proximity to the airport reveals

that neighboring residential areas and schools suffer most from noise.

In constrast, pollution is a city wide problem which endangers the health

of the entire greater Boston community. The airport must be situated so

as to minimize the influence of these unfavorable by-products upon
particular communities and upon the city as a whole.

Given this limitation, certain areas of the city would appear
more receptive to use than others. One also hopes to balance the costs
and benefits of an airport to the locality. Sections which generate the
prime airport use should contribute most to its needs. The people who
frequently avail themselves of air transportation most enjoy its presence.
Those who have no occasion to fly realize only the secondary benefits
of cargo and mail delivered, employment and servicing contracts.

## 3.10    The Airport at Present

Boston's present airport situation appears quite simple. The
airport lies close to the city center and to many residential tracts. Demand
is growing for expanded air services. The continuation of present policy
means that residents of nearby communities will pay further costs. The
well-established community of East Boston suffers particularly. Each
successive expansion brings noise and pollution closer to the doorsteps
of its 40,000 residents. Few inhabitants of this lower-middle class
community use airline service regularly, but at least Logan is a major
employer of East Boston workers. A variety of reasons continue to make
residents reluctant to move, yet anger is clearly expressed at present
disturbance, not to mention the possibility of further expansion. Object-
ively, one cannot say that residents receive a good return on their
continued  investment of taxes and tolerance. The more prosperous

communities which would willingly finance expansion understandably

hesitate to locate the airport any nearer to their own homes fearing the

effects of noise, pollution, and traffic.

This is but one instance of a nearly universal difficulty one

faces when building or expanding an airport. Lacking any large open

space near the city, one must displace a settled community. When the

area is a tight-knit ethnic entity such as East Boston, relocation of the

entire unit becomes as essential as it is unlikely. The fear that moving

will destroy community patterns and group traditions induces citizens

not only to tolerate sinking real estate values and disturbance, but to

resist further encroachments into their neighborhood. Local legislators

seize their moment and denounce further expansion at the expense of the

public[5] and the ensuing struggle further unifies the community.

---

[5]      " Mr. Chairman, let me take a moment to illustrate the unwieldy
and devious methods used by the M.P.A.
        Three years ago we were told by the M.P.A. that all we need is
this small parcel of land near Jeffries Point, and we will be satisfied.
        Two years ago we were told by the M.P.A., all we need is the
extension of Runway 15-33 into Wood Island Park and we will be satisfied.
        Last year we were told all we want is the land owned and occupied by
36 families and a gas station and we will be satisfied.
        This year we are told that all we want is to extend certain runways
toward Winthrop, build an additional runway 2,000 feet closer to Winthrop
parallel to 15-33 and we need more land toward East Boston and again we
will be satisfied.
        Mr. Chairman, I submit to you that this monster that we created has
an unquenchable thirst for more land, more than we can afford to give
without jeopardizing one million people.

              Rep. R.E. Siriani before the Joint Committee on Transportation,
              Legislature of the Commonwealth of Massachusetts, April, 1967.

As a planner one may choose one of two directions. One may
assume (perhaps rightly) that these people will continue to tolerate
future escalation of these adverse conditions. When each individual
reaches his limit of endurance he will find a home elsewhere, grumble
loudly about his treatment at the hands of the M.P.A., and probably
do nothing more. Or the airport administration can plan to pay for an
equitable solution to the problem: either in the form of a realistic and
acceptable, but restricted alternative, or a new plan that will circum-
vent further social hardship.

This study, in any event, hopes to explore how and why
community-airport frictions develop and from this background to
indicate ways of avoiding similar situations as the demands of air
service grow. A primary conclusion is that neglect of consideration of
community cohesiveness and make-up ends in unanticipated protest
and blind destruction.

## 3.11    Noise

America is the noisiest nation in the world; the land surrounding
airports is among the most noise plagued in the country. All of us
frequently perceive the truth of this statement, but to ameliorate a
serious situation we need measures and definable quantities. How
noisy is it, and what are the primary adverse effects of this noise?
It can be fairly stated that by and large planners of the past have not
attended to this problem. Most airports in use today were planned

and constructed well in advance of the jet age, in a day when it may have

been fashionable to watch the silver birds whir to a landing. Since 1958,

the beginning of the jet age in commercial aviation, occasional annoyance

with noise has metamorphosed into steady outrage. Each year the number

of flights leaving and arriving hourly rises, magnifying the degree of

noise pollution. Social interaction at schools, churches, and homes is

interrupted as often as once a minute. Finally, with the economic maturity

of air cargo transportation, night flights have swelled insomniac ranks

many times over.

The noise issues directly from the aircraft engines, and because

engines must power take-offs and landings, the sound can only stop if

one suspends jet service. Technological advances in reducing the level

of noise will be discussed later in this chapter, but simply stated, the

noise is created by the movement of vast quantities of air through the

jet engine. As aircraft size and weight increase, so then does the engine

power, the energy demands, and therefore, the noise. Little hope is held

for the substantial reduction of noise below levels tolerated at airports

today, although there is optimism that present levels can be maintained

with all future aircraft. The noise problem must partially determine the

design and location of any new air facility in the immediate, and most

probably, distant future.

Noise, which may be defined as unwanted sound, is not solely

a function of physical loudness; it is also true that "there apparently

is a basic (and presumably unlearned) unwantedness or noisiness to sound beyond that due solely to its loudness."[6] Thus, noisiness increases

at a faster rate than loudness as:

1) the pitch of sound increases

2) the complexity of the spectrum increases

3) the duration increases (beyond 200 milliseconds)

4) the frequency with which one hears the noise increases.

In an attempt to quantify noise disturbance a measure has been

developed relating the discomfort perceived to the noise intensity,

duration, and frequency. The unit of measure is Perceived Noise Decibels

(PNdB). Using it, one can define a proximity limit around the approach

paths in which it is intolerable to live. A secondary limit is the area in

which people find the noise objectionable but tolerable. Noise contours,

as such limits are termed, can be developed for any type of aircraft

and frequency of use.

We present the following example as a concrete illustration of the

use of PNdB of aircraft and of another noise concept, the CNR (Composite

Noise Rating.) A 727 jet aircraft at 1500 feet produces a peak PNdB level

of 105 outdoors and 89 indoors for about 25 seconds. 32 such occurences

during the hours of 7 a.m. to 10 p.m. are sufficient to achieve a CNR

of 100. An F.A.A. publication in 1964 estimates that a CNR of 100 to 115

may result in vigorous individual complaint (Table 3.1), and perhaps,

---

[6] <u>Alleviation of Jet Aircraft Noise Near Airports</u>, Report of the Jet Aircraft
Noise Panel, Science and Technology Office, Executive Office of the
President, The Government Printing Office, Washington, D.C., March,
1966, page

| Composite Noise Rating | | Zone | Description of Expected Response |
|---|---|---|---|
| Take-offs and Landings | Runups | | |
| Less Than 100 | Less Than 80 | 1 | Essentially no complaints would be expected. The noise may, however, interfere occasionally with certain activities |
| 100 to 115 | 80 to 95 | 2 | Individuals may complain, perhaps vigorously. Concerted group action is possible. |
| Greater Than 115 | Greater Than 95 | 3 | Individual reactions would likely include repeated, vigorous complaints. Concerted group action might be expected. |

Table 3.1 Anticipated Response to CNR Levels[7]

concerted group action[8]. 1500 feet is the typical altitude of an aircraft 3 miles from the start of take-off.

Noise contours appear in Figure 3.3 for Logan Airport's present configuration. Their oval shape reflects the approach and take-off patterns of the runways. One may associate a noise pattern with any type of aircraft operating at a stated power output. This pattern can be represented as contours of equal noise level which completely surround the aircraft. As a plane approaches the airport and drops lower and lower, this noise "ground shadow"

---

[7] Bolt, Beranek, and Newman, Inc., Land Use Planning Relating to Aircraft Noise, the F.A.A., Washington, D.C., October, 1964, page 12.
[8] Ibid., page 14.

increases in size as the shapes in Figure 3.3 illustrate.  As can be seen,

Figure 3.3 Logan Airport Noise Contour

Logan's noise problem is of some magnitude.  Approximately 30,000

people in East Boston and Winthrop live within the intolerable range
and 100,000 more in the objectionable range. Naturally, the noise is
tolerated to different degrees by different social functions (Table 3.2).
For example, an air conditioned industrial plant would be hard pressed
to distinguish between its own noise and the noise of approaching aircraft, while a school or library...

3.12   Pollution

The pollution problem by no means occupies a central position
in the location decision. Nonetheless, it can be regarded as a valid
criterion to be considered in the decision-making process. Like noise,
air pollution is an unwanted side effect of airports. The question is:
to what extent is pollution a problem and how much weight should be
attached to it?

Unlike most airports, Logan is situated in the middle of the city
and it, therefore, adds to the over-all pollution problem. Absolute figures
on pollution are readily obtainable. For each 1000 gallons of fuel consumed by a jet aircraft, the following amounts of pollutants are discharged:

| | |
|---|---|
| Carbon Monoxide | 56 lbs. |
| Hydrocarbons | 15 lbs. |
| Nitrogen Oxides | 37 lbs. |
| Particles (Dirt) | 54 lbs. |
| Aldehydes | 6 lbs. |

Some 500,000 gallons of fuel[9] are consumed every day at Logan Airport

[9] According to figures obtained from Representative Ralph Siriani. Although
Siriani is from Winthrop and one of his prime objectives is the creation
of a second airport, we have no reason to disbelieve these figures.

| Noise Sensitivity Zone | Composite Noise Rating (CNR) Take offs & Landings | Residential | Commercial | Hotel, Motel | Offices, Public Buildings | Schools, Hospitals, Churches | Theatres, Auditoriums | Outdoor Amphitheaters, Theaters | Outdoor Recreational (Non-Spectator) | Industrial |
|---|---|---|---|---|---|---|---|---|---|---|
| I | Under 90 | y | y | y | y | y | A | A | y | y |
| II | 90-100 | y | y | y | y | C | C | n | y | y |
| III | 100-115 | B | y | C | C | n | n | n | y | y |
| IV | Over 115 | n | C | n | n | n | n | n | y | C |

KEY     y - yes; n - no
A - A detailed noise analysis by qualified personnel should be undertaken for all indoor or outdoor music auditoriums and all outdoor theaters.
B - Case history experience indicates that individuals in private residences may complain, perhaps vigorously. Concerted group action is possible. New single dwelling construction should generally be avoided. For high density dwellings (apartments) construction, C will apply.
C - Avoid construction unless a detailed analysis of noise reduction requirements is made and needed noise control features are included in building design.

Table 3.2 Viability of Community Activities
and Industries in 4 CNR Level Zones[10]

[10]Bolt, Beranek, and Newman, "Analysis of Community and Airport Relationships/ Noise Abatement," Dec. 1965, AD 645 955.

and in the immediate vicinity.  Therefore, some 84,000 lbs. of contaminants

are discharged into the air in and near Boston every day.

These figures, however, deceive us if we have no idea of other

factors that contribute to the problem.  Fortunately, some figures are

available.  From Restoring the Quality of Our Environment[11], we gathered

some figures on the daily release of contaminants into the air in Phila-

delphia.  Admittedly, Philadelphia is not Boston, but a useful first-order

approximation should be possible.  According to the report, the following

amounts of pollutants are released daily in  Philadelphia:

> 830 tons of Sulphur Dioxide
> 300 tons of Nitrogen Oxides
> 1350 tons of Hydrocarbons
> 470 tons of Particles

If these figures rather than  Representative Siriani's figures are accepted

as a basis, we find that the following percentages of contaminants are

contributed by jet aircraft in Boston:

> 3.08%  Nitrogen Oxides
> .30%  Hydrocarbons
> 2.80%  Particles

Compared to the dimensions of the whole problem, these figures

are hardly frightening, but deserve consideration in an over-all analysis.

---

[11] The Environmental Pollution Panel of the President's Science Advisory
Committee, "Restoring the Quality of Our Environment," U.S. Government
Printing Office, Washington, D.C., November, 1965.

Chapter **4**

SITE SELECTION: SOLUTIONS

## 4.1 V/STOL and the Demand for Improved Short-Haul Transport

A concept widely discussed for some 25 years may be the key to improving future air transportation while minimizing community disturbance. STOL and VTOL aircraft are neither flashy nor extraordinarily fast, but are particularly suited to short-haul flights[1]. They operate relatively noise-lessly compared to fixed-wing craft and require only short runways. A system consisting largely of V/STOL operation could offer ideal service for a city such as Boston in which the dominant demand is for short-haul transport. Figure 4.1 illustrates three V/STOL concepts appropriate for short-haul networks.

To determine V/STOL relative efficiency and desirability, one must examine over-all time and cost figures for short-haul flights using present CTOL vehicles. Currently, these figures are distinctly unimpressive. One wastes a great deal of time and money in getting to and from the airport,

---

[1] A short-haul trip is defined as a trip of less than 300 miles.

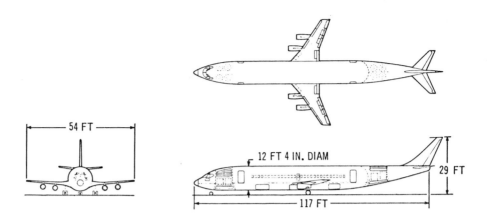

*Jet Lift VTOL—120-Passenger Capacity*

VERTICAL TAKEOFF IS ACCOMPLISHED WITH THE USE OF EIGHT AUXILIARY LIFT ENGINES IN
THE BODY, PLUS THE DEFLECTED THRUST OF THE FOUR CRUISE ENGINES. CONTROL IN THE
VERTICAL MODE IS BY DIFFERENTIAL ENGINE THRUST. THE HIGH WING LOADING ALLOWS
SMOOTH, EFFICIENT HIGH SPEED CRUISE.

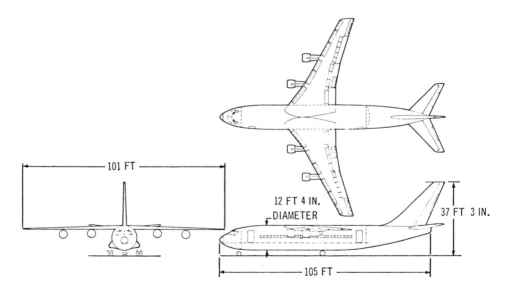

*High Lift STOL—120-Passenger Capacity*

EXTERNALLY BLOWN FLAPS ARE THE RELATIVELY SIMPLE HIGH LIFT DEVICES USED TO
OBTAIN STOL PERFORMANCE. THE AFT SEGMENT OF THE INBOARD FLAPS ARTICULATE
WITH THROTTLE MOVEMENT TO PROVIDE GLIDE PATH CONTROL. TWO DIFFERENT DESIGN
WING LOADINGS ARE USED WITH THIS CONCEPT TO PROVIDE TWO DIFFERENT DESIGN FIELD
LENGTHS.

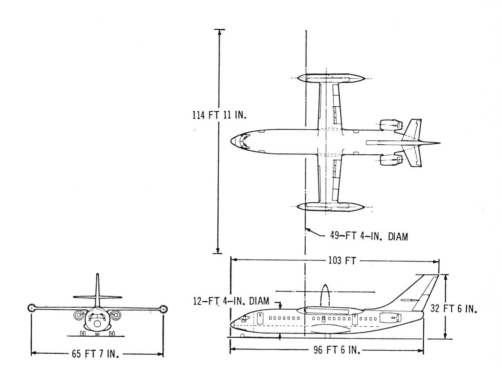

*Folding Tilt Rotor VTOL—120-Passenger Capacity*

LIFT IS SUPPLIED BY THE ROTORS DURING HOVER AND TRANSITION. FOR CONVENTIONAL
FLIGHT THE ROTORS ARE FEATHERED, STOPPED AND THE BLADES FOLDED REARWARD
INTO WING TIP NACELLES. CONVERTIBLE FAN ENGINES PROVIDE SHAFT POWER FOR THE
ROTOR DRIVE SYSTEM AND CONVERT TO GIVE FAN THRUST FOR THE CONVENTIONAL FLIGHT
MODE.

Figure 4.1 Three Boeing V/STOL Concepts

---

[1] <u>Study of Aircraft in Short-Haul Transportation Systems</u>, prepared by the
Boeing Corp. for NASA, Washington, D.C., January, 1968, NASA Contract
Report CR-986.

having baggage handled, obtaining tickets and waiting for the plane. Since New York is the predominant destination of Boston short-haul flights, we will use it as our primary example of present air service trip times and costs.

The SARC[2] report on intercity passenger travel offers a detailed breakdown of the total trip time and costs from New York to Boston. The report takes percentages of access trips by various modes and presents figures for average cost and access time to Boston and New York ports. The access modes averaged are car, taxi, limousine, and public transportation. For Boston, the average trip from home to the airport takes 38 minutes and costs $2.66; from downtown the trip takes 32 minutes at a cost of $1.45. For New York, the figures are from home 51 minutes at $3.50 and from downtown 52 minutes costing $2.75. When one adds these times to an average plane trip time of 50 minutes plus a typical 15 minute delay an average CTOL plane trip requires 2 hours and 34 minutes for home to home and 2 hours and 29 minutes for town to town. Access costs added to the $18.00 coach fare give us costs of $24.16 for home to home and $22.20 for downtown Boston to downtown New York City.

These high totals, which clearly reflect high access costs, in terms of money and especially of valuable time, can be expected to increase still further since access times in densely populated regions will continue to soar.

_____

[2] Systems Analysis and Research Corp., "Demand for Intercity Passenger Travel in the Washington-Boston Corridor", Boston, Mass., 1963.

In Boston, the estimated 50% net increase in population in the next 20 years will occur outside the core area[3]. For people living outside the core, the average trip time to Logan is now 65 minutes. Therefore, the average access time in 20 years, barring a sudden development in rapid ground transport and assuming that highway construction keeps pace with the growth of traffic, will be 47 minutes.

From the SARC report one may deduce not only the inefficiency of the current CTOL air service, but also the superiority of even this level of service to all competing modes for trips of more than several hours. While improvement of the major long-haul contender, rail service in the Corridor, is currently under consideration, it is too early to predict that significant improvement in this mode will occur. Improved rail systems may attract some proportion of potential air service customers but it seems probable that even significantly improved rail service will not compete vigorously with the growing air market.

Demonstrations are now in progress utilizing lightweight turbine powered trains between Boston and New York. These trains take 3 hours and 55 minutes because their speed is restricted by the characteristics of the existing track. The trip time could be reduced to less than 3 hours if a major program of track upgrading were undertaken. Even a 55 minute reduction in rail travel time would significantly reduce the time saved

---

[3] Transportation Facts for the Boston Region, 2nd Ed., The B.R.A., Boston, Massachusetts, 1968, pp. 29-33.

when one travels by air. Consequently, if air fare were to remain the same,
the amount of time one could still save should be costed at a higher hourly
rate. As a result, the institution of three-hour rail service could further
increase the pressure for air fare reductions. Rail may win back some of
the market it has lost, possibly up to 500,000 short-haul trips per year.
Nevertheless, even the realization of this rail traffic would not greatly
diminish the short-haul air market.

The second type of new rail-like system is the High Speed Ground
Transportation (HSGT) System which is being studied by several groups,
including one at M.I.T. These studies propose regional guideway systems
in conjunction with multiple terminals designed to minimize access problems.
Such systems could lower present minimum short-haul times but as cited
by the M.I.T. report[4], most proposals admit ignorance in three areas:
technology, cost reduction, and public exposure. Due to their extreme
cost and current rudimentary stage of development, in all likelihood a
sophisticated HSGT System will not be achieved within thirty or forty
years. Therefore competition from HSGT will probably not be formidable;
short-haul air transportation will therefore feel no noticable effects
within the period for which meaningful traffic projections can be made.

Trends in conventional air, auto, bus, and rail travel, as well
as future economic factors, have been included in models which can

---

[4] Survey of Technology for High Speed Ground Transport, prepared by M.I.T.
for the U.S. Dept.of Commerce, Washington, D.C., Contract No. C-85-65,
(PB 168 648), June 15, 1965.

predict air travel in the next few decades. In 1980, the Stanford report[5] projects 2,330,000 passenger trips to New York from Boston, 515,000 trips to Washington, and 415,000 trips to Philadelphia. Significant technological advances, such as the adoption of an efficient V/STOL system or the advent of high speed rail travel, will, in turn, create deviations from these figures.

Finally, the demand for a new or improved short-haul system is seen in six present truths. First, people want to obtain the fastest and most convenient type of travel, as the growing preference for air service attests. Second, the businessman, the greatest traveler, consents to spend a fair amount to save trip time. Third, and most important, the present system is not efficient. From time and cost figures, one sees that access takes a disproportionate amount of time and money. Fourth, a megalopolis is presently being forged in the Northeast Corridor with attendant problems of mobility, since a unified region demands an integrated transportation system. Fifth, Boston spreads in its growth; all growth in the next 20 years will take place outside the core area. An efficient system joining all parts of the metropolitan area is therefore vital. Sixth, people in smaller cities near major ports, such as Worcester, contribute notably to the demand for intercity travel.

---

[5] An Economic Analysis of Commercial VTOL and STOL Transport Aircraft, prepared by the Stanford Research Institute for the F.A.A., Washington, D.C., Contract No. FA-64 WA-4997, February 1966.

4.2     VTOL and STOL Preliminary System

A complete V/STOL (Verticle/Short Take-Off and Landing) network,
the logical choice for a new system, cannot be developed immediately for
a number of reasons. Preliminary costs are high. Parallel development
must occur in cities other than Boston; then, the system must grow with
demand. The Stanford report, however, outlines a limited system which
can function efficiently and be transformed in time into a sophisticated
system.

To determine demand for V/STOL service, the Stanford report
calculates for each city what it labels the "convenience factor". To
arrive at the "convenience factor" for Boston one adds to the percentage
of passengers who leave or depart from downtown Boston the percentage
of those who would rather leave (or enter) Boston via a downtown terminal.
For Boston, 12% and 70% are the respective estimates, and hence the
"convenience factor" is 82%. Other "convenience factors" are 48% for
New York, 88% for Washington, and 70% for Philadelphia. These figures
lead the Stanford Report to make a primary assumption that each major
city will welcome a V/STOL port near the downtown area. The small size
of V/STOL ports makes this premise reasonable.

The report then discusses the traffic between any two cities, or
any "city pair". Stanford formulates the "city pair penetration factor",
the product of the convenience factors for the two cities involved. The
Boston-New York factor is 39%, the Boston-Washington factor is 72%,
the the Boston-Philadelphia factor is 57%. One assumes that V/STOL

has a market potential equal to the "city pair penetration factor" times
the total air market. This assumption yields a potential for V/STOL flights
out of Boston to New York, Washington, and Philadelphia of 3,714 passenger
trips per day in 1975 and 4,154 per day in 1980, or respectively 1,355,400
and 1,516,750 per year.

In Chapter VI of the Stanford report, consideration turns to aircraft
capable of carrying from 40 to 100 passengers by 1975 and 1980 and esti-
mations are made of fares and schedule frequencies for proposed aircraft.
To operate at 10% profit, feasible 60-passenger craft must demand fares
smaller than the desired competitive fares, yet not a great deal higher
then established fares for conventional craft. The 60-passenger plane
is desirable from the point of view of schedules between certain city pairs.
For 100-passenger flights, less than conventional fares may be charged
in some cases. For the Boston-New York market, the volume of traffic
permits planes with 100 passengers to yield efficient service. The projected
Boston-New York fare for the 100-passenger VT-2 model is $18.99, for
the 60-passenger model, $21.88. By 1975, the time to New York will be
one hour as compared to 2 hours and 38 minutes by CTOL craft and 3 hours
and 20 minutes by rail. The value of the 1 hour and 38 minutes saving to
a passenger whose time is worth $3.50 per hour is $5.72. If the fare-
differential for the V/STOL trip is less than $5.72 this passenger would
presumably choose V/STOL.

For the Boston-Washington trip the Stanford report projects a time
saving of 0:46 and $2.68, for Boston-Philadelphia 1:19 and $4.61. These

smaller time savings achieved by V/STOL as compared with CTOL reflect
the greater distance between Boston and these destinations; fare differentials must be greater for the same reason. V/STOL operation particularly to Washington would undoubedly run at fares with an increment greater
than $2.68. A passenger whose time is worth $3.50 an hour might find
that he was spending considerably in excess of that amount for the time
saved. One can therefore postulate that little of the Boston-Washington
V/STOL will be reached, while a good part of the Boston-Philadelphia
traffic will be handled in 10 years by V/STOL.

The Stanford system serves as an efficient stepping-stone to a
more sophisticated network to be instituted later. That certain trips do
not appear feasible in 1980 does not diminish their likelihood in 1985 or
1990. A sophisticated system which capitalizes on growing V/STOL
potential will return greater profits. A system with one port per city
simply answers interium needs and reflects interim conditions.

The Stanford report outlines a very basic V/STOL system, an
initial break with conventional short-haul air transportation. The report
takes a basically conservative view, conservative in its technological
predictions and cautious in its economic analysis and forecasts. This
approach is, in a sense, advisable for the introduction of V/STOL which
will find itself, like so many other innovations, handicapped by skepticism.
Even such reservations do not prevent the Stanford report from concluding
that the rudimentary system of one downtown port in Boston for travel to
New York and Philadelphia will achieve substantial profits and an effec-

tiveness that can only promote general acceptance of the V/STOL concepts.

4.3     V/STOL Advanced Network

A study produced by Boeing[6] at the request of NASA looks beyond

the Stanford report. It analyzes in some detail the possibilities of a

complex V/STOL network in three distinct regions of the United States,

including Boston's Northeast Corridor. This report investigates the

relative suitability of the various VTOL, STOL and CTOL concepts around

1985. Actually, by assuming a certain amount of technological and economic

growth derived from a postulated V/STOL system, the Boeing study projects

a "second generation" system. Boeing deems likely that by 1985 the

various concepts of V/STOL craft discussed in the report will be operative

and technologically "mature" (a feeling not shared by the authors of the

Stanford report.) They further predicate that the V/STOL concept will be

fully accepted by the passenger market and, in fact, will have stimulated

growth in market demand. Lastly, Boeing accepts, as given, promotion

by federal, state, and local agencies and consequent parallel growth of

the system in all specified port-cities. These assumptions are consider-

able but, reviewing the Stanford report we see that barring a sudden dis-

enchantment with V/STOL craft or the miraculous emergence of a super-

rapid ground system, the adoption of a highly developed V/STOL system

must occur in time---be it in 1985 or 1995. Thus, we can regard the Boeing

---

[6] The Study of Aircraft in Short-Haul Transportation Systems, prepared by
the Boeing Co. for NASA, Washington, D.C., NASA CR-986, January 1968.

model as the sophisticated system envisaged in the Stanford report and
by the same token, see the fundamental Stanford system as the initial
system predicted by Boeing, the only possible discrepancy being that
of time.

Boeing's economic analysis of V/STOL transportation opens with
an evaluation of market demand in 1985. Their traffic forecasting model
utilizes the factors of gross national product, absolute price of air travel,
general price level, size of the labor force, and quality of air travel and
service improvement. This model, applied to the thirty year period between
1936 and 1966, yields very satisfactory results. Boeing then makes projections to 1985, again with certain assumptions about the trends in GNP,
average cost per seat mile of flight, maximum speed, and other "residual
forces". This study predicts an 8.7-fold increase in revenue passenger
miles for the U.S. domestic scheduled air carriers from 51.8 billion in
1965 to 450 billion in 1985. To compile the final demand figures for
various city pairs, Boeing looks at statistics from 1949 through 1966 which
show that the percentages of total U.S. domestic flights between almost
all major cities is a remarkably constant figure. They then predict how
demand in 1985 will be distributed throughout the various U.S. cities.

This model yields an extremely high demand for air traffic between
Boston and New York City (16 million passengers per year for 1985), Boston
and Washington (3 million), and Boston and Philadelphia (2 million), a
demand level much higher than that previously cited.

The Boeing study considers nine different VTOL, STOL and CTOL concepts. It does not, however, make any sweeping conclusions about the superiority of any particular VTOL or STOL craft. Although it does suggest certain criteria, such as range, which will eventually aid one to distinguish individual design concepts, by and large the report presents an analysis of the relative effectiveness of V/STOL craft as a group compared with CTOL craft.

As indicated previously, V/STOL craft enjoy the obvious advantage of maneuverability, therefore ability to land in areas too small for conventional aircraft. This feature enables travel direct "city center" to "city center" and "suburb" to "city center". Thereby the traveler enjoys savings in time and consequently savings in money.

The total cost of a trip for the passenger comprises explicit costs (plane fare plus access costs) and implicit costs (the money value he places on his time). One assumes that the traveler will try to minimize his total transportation costs. Thus, if two modes of transportation have the same explicit costs, the one that is faster will have the lower total cost (since, as we have shown, the average traveler attaches some money value to his time).

With this in mind, the Boeing report chose to analyze the economic feasibility of V/STOL concepts bearing the same explicit costs as the CTOL crafts, thus taking a slightly different approach than did the Stanford group. To the V/STOL fare set at the CTOL fare level, they added a premium increment equal to the differential due to the savings in access costs provided by the former. They relied upon reduced access times to make the V/STOL method of travel attractive. The Boeing study shows the

total average access costs to and from a CTOL port to be $6.00, the total

for a suburban V/STOL port to be $4.33, and that for a downtown VTOL

port to be $4.00. Thus, the access cost differential is from $1.67 to

$2.00 over the CTOL fare. This method of fare determination works well

since it does not rely upon a specific CTOL fare level but can adjust

according to changes in CTOL fares. For 1985, the base CTOL fare is

estimated roughly at $7.00 for a Boston-New York trip; this enormous

reduction from the Stanford figure stems largely from predicted increased

capacity of CTOL aircraft.

The Boeing report analyzes three sizes of aircraft for all concepts,

200, 120, and 90 passenger capacities, a significant size increase in

assumed technological sophistication over the vehicles discussed in the

Stanford report. Using the "indifference fare level", the profitability of

the V/STOL concepts is compared with that of CTOL craft. Boeing desig-

nates return on sales (ROS) as the profitability criterion because it is

easily understood and widely accepted. While today's operations over

similar routes have not been especially profitable, for future operations

approximately 10% ROS after taxes would represent a reasonable target.

When V/STOL fares are based upon the fares of large conventional

aircraft, at all ranges (100-400 miles) the 200 passenger V/STOL craft

is more profitable than comparable size CTOL craft. For flights between

New York and Boston the profit as a percent of sales would be approximately

12% for CTOL and 17% for certain V/STOL concepts. Even for the longer haul between Washington and Boston, STOL craft and even certain VTOL

craft would show higher profits than CTOL planes (15%, 14%, and 13%

respectively), thus indicating an added "longer-haul" market that the

original system fails to capture. For smaller capacity aircraft (120 passen-

gers) the return on sales naturally decreases, but the relative greater

profitability of V/STOL still remains for both short and longer ranges

(10% ROS for V/STOL between New York and Boston as compared with 6%

for CTOL, and 7% ROS for V/STOL between Washington and Boston as

compared with 6% for CTOL). Thus, from the airlines' point of view,

the economic feasibility of V/STOL craft has been shown. If the V/STOL

"explicit" fares can match the CTOL "explicit" fares then the time saved

flying V/STOL will certainly create a V/STOL "monopoly" on the short-

haul market. Rough estimates of access times to various CTOL and V/STOL

terminals indicate a savings of 30 to 45 minutes for trips to both New York

and Washington from Boston. For a businessman paid by the hour who

frequently travels these routes, this savings can amount to sizable sums.

V/STOL crafts also appear to relative advantage in terms of noise

output. Smaller take-off and landing areas allow these planes to emit

their blanket of noise over a reduced area. Noise level may be decreased

even further if one employs elevated landing pads (for example at the

top of terminal buildings).

Having brought forth all this economic data, the Boeing report

proceeds to propose specific V/STOL systems for major cities, including

Boston. Allocation of terminals in terms of efficient access, demands, and scheduling considerations dictates four V/STOL terminals for Boston

at an approximate cost of $20 to $30 million each. Boeing suggests

terminals in the following locations: two "city center" ports in the

railroad yards, one on the Charles River and one at the South Bay, and

two "suburban" terminals in the Route 128 region. Variations on the

Boeing proposals might be V/STOL ports right at Logan and possibly

movement or addition of one to the growing region around Route I-495.

These four terminals will handle a total of 243 departures and the same

number of arrivals per day in 1985: 120 to and from New York, 40 to

Washington, 32 to Philadelphia, 24 to Baltimore, and lesser numbers to

Albany, Syracuse, Providence, and Hartford. The four terminals will,

of course, split the load to insure maximum scheduling convenience for

the passengers while maintaining minimum terminal traffic. Each port

will offer between 100 to 140 total flights a day allowing all possible

"city" and "suburban" combinations. This spread system boasts obvious

advantages; the decrease in access times with no corresponding increase

in cost will cause the V/STOL system to prosper.

## 4.4    Noise Solutions

The maximum tolerable noise level differs slightly between

individuals and may even vary from community to community. The Port

Authority of New York has set a maximum noise level in adjacent

communities of 112 PNdB. A great deal of hostility has thereby been

engendered in the New York area. Some communities have engaged themselves in legal action against the noise levels since the days of

propeller aircraft; the number of lawsuits has soared since the advent

of the jets. This would indicate "that a significant number of people

find that a distribution of aircraft noise levels... is unacceptable to

them"[7]. The United States Jet Aircraft Noise Panel therefore recommends

the establishment of peak levels at 100 PNdB in the report from which the

above quotation is taken.

From the area near Logan, particularly, though not exclusively,

East Boston, there has issued a steady stream of individual complaints,

and threats of concerted community action against the Massachusetts

Port Authority. Not all of these complaints concern the noise problem;

indeed, residents feel more disturbed about the loss of land to the M.P.A.

Yet the noise problem remains serious and it is growing.

The noise level may be kept down by several possible methods.

Some ideas suggested are:

1) Developing quieter engines

2) Setting curfews on arriving and departing planes

3) Utilizing two stage take-off procedures

4) Restricting turns on take-offs and landings

5) Establishing artifical buffer zones around airports

---

[7] *Alleviation of Jet Aircraft Noise Near Airports*, Report of the Jet Aircraft
Noise Panel, Science and Technology Office, Executive Office of the
President, the Government Printing Office, Washington, D.C., March
1966, page 21.

6) Zoning near-by areas

7) Acquiring land near airports

8) Sound-proofing neighboring houses

9) Utilizing alternate airports for night and/or cargo and/or long-haul operations

Several of these noise abatement procedures are now in use at airports around the country. Practically speaking, the last four procedures appear most useful for reducing noise levels to a tolerable range. Depending on the location of the airport and near-by communities, one may employ a combination of measures to achieve this end.

If we consider the peak load for a projected Boston airport in 1990, we can identify three important noise areas:

1) An area within which residential use of land would be impossible

2) An area within which residential use of land would be possible but difficult

3) An area within which the noise level would be significant but not detrimental to residential use of land

The first area would involve the necessary relocation of all dwelling units and residents. The problems and costs are considered in Section 3.5, Chapter 3, on relocation. With the second area, however, we begin to come to grips with the problem of noise levels. Here, the exterior noise level (CNR) may be compatible with various land uses, homes, offices, hotels, even schools. The interior noise levels, however, are not. Depending on the site chosen for an airport, this problem could be overcome by any of the last four methods. In highly populated areas, however, only sound proofing is a suitable solution.

At this point it could be argued that, as at present, nothing need be done for such residents. This view, we, as planners, reject. Whatever the system adopted, all ramifications must be considered. Following this line of thought, we consider the third area. Here noise levels are " tolerable" but the added noise must certainly be a discomfiture for residents.

We have attempted to place a cost figure on the noise problem in the second area by estimating the number of dwelling units in the area and multiplying it by the average cost of sound proofing. This figure does not include the costs of ventilation and/or air conditioning of each unit; it also does not include the costs of sound proofing non-residential units: e.g. offices, stores, or schools. Yet it does give some idea of the cost of noise.

In the third area, it is more difficult to associate a cost figure with the problem since nothing concrete need be done for residents. Yet, it is clear the following is the order of site preferability, based on the criterion of noise:

1) Brewster - so situated in the harbor that the outer noise perimeter barely touches the land.
2) Duxbury - jutting out into the ocean with runways facing toward the sea, by and large; noise problem only slightly greater than Brewster's.
3) Harvard - noise would affect neighboring towns of Stow, Maynard, and Hudson.
4) Hanscomb - would disturb some 60,000 people in near-by built-up suburbs.
5) Logan - would affect up to 100,000 people along the coast as far as Lynn and inland to Chelsea.

4.5     Computer Modeling

The major parameters which influence a passenger's choice of mode are convenience, speed, reliability, and cost, although for each person the relative importance of these factors varies with the purpose of his trip, the value of his time, and individual preferences. Of course each of the above further implies certain functions; convenience comprises frequency of service; speed demands accessible terminals. Future demand for passenger and cargo air transport can only be estimated if one possesses a general awareness of these parameters as well as knowledge of future technological possibilities.

As the above indicates, the process of modeling a dynamic system begins with an analysis of transport system components and their interactions, as well as a look at influential policies. These elements are then employed as follows. One introduces past airport situation models into the computer; it produces a resulting present situation. Then by readjusting factor laodings until an accurate model of the present situation is achieved, one can construct a realistic mechanism which will predict future transportation demand levels. Control as well as prediction is possible since a change in policies can adjust performance to the standards desired.

Figure 4.2 pictures the model built to predict demand for airport facilities. The inputs are population, industry, and transients, transients being users whose trip originates in another city. These three groups determine the passenger base. Reputation acts like a hand on a faucet

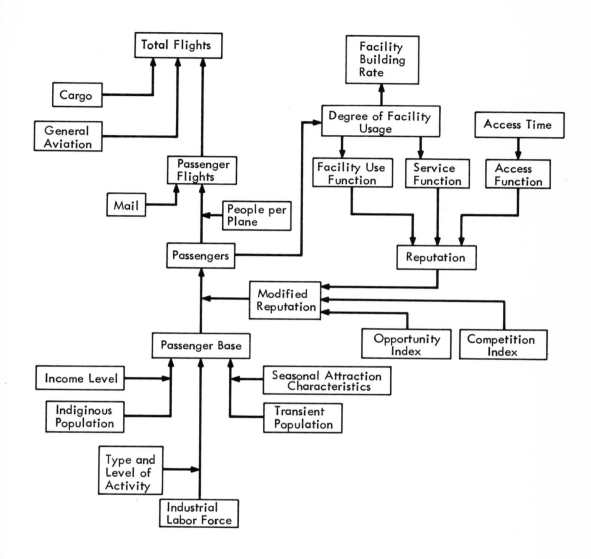

Figure 4.2 Airport Demand Prediction Model

controlling the rate of flow. As reputation improves, the flow into the

passenger base swells and appropriate growth occurs in the airport

facilities.

Reputation derives from three sources: access time, average terminal delay time, and the extent of facility use. As the former two decrease, reputation improves; the flow into the passenger base swells. However, as greater than 75% of the facilities are in use at one time, desirability will wane due to crowding. Appropriate growth in airport facilities must then occur.

Within our model we manipulated factors such as the size of facilities and access time to determine resulting use and terminal delays. We found that a 30 minute supplement of access time would diminish demand 8%, while a 60 minute increase would provoke a 20% decline. We judged that access time above 40 minutes begins to seriously shrink demand, a conclusion to remember when choosing an airport location.

We constructed our model utilizing industrial dynamics methodology, a technique developed at M.I.T. by Professors Jay Forrester and Alexander Pugh. Industrial dynamics uses a digital computer language called DYNAMO[8] to transform the system components into system behavior. The language, and hence the model, is based upon mathematical interpretation of the system, essentially in linear terms, although nonlinearities may be introduced in the form of curves.

We present the computer's demand predictions in the form of several time curves. Figure 4.3 represents projected annual passenger demand from

---

[8] Pugh, Alexander L. III, <u>DYNAMO User's Manual</u>, 2nd Ed., M.I.T. Press, Cambridge, Mass., 1963.

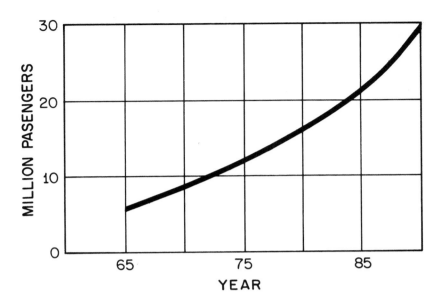

Figure 4.3  Dynamic Model Predicted Air Travel Demand

1965 to 1990, our design target.  As can be seen from the curve, 8.5 million

people use Logan airport annually at this time.  The projection indicates that

in 1990, approximately 28 million passengers will use the airport facilities

in the Boston area.

We include in our factor loadings statements about anticipated facilities.

We have assumed that prospective passengers will have the convenience of

three short-haul embarkation points and a single major long-haul air terminal.

The grounds for this assumption will be clarified in subsequent discussion.

Figure 4.4 illustrates the demand for each category of service at present,

at the time of our design, and during the intervening time.  The curves indicate

the effects on trade demand differences of the number of aircraft operations the

airport must handle.  Note that cargo flights wax nearly fourfold, reaching 11,250

flights per month by 1990; this reflects substantial rise in the cargo tonnage being shipped annually; from the 72,000 tons per month handled in 1967 we expect a

rise to almost 1 million tons per month in 1990, a fourteenfold increase. More

efficient cargo handling methods and larger, better designed aircraft hopefully

will help to keep the number of air cargo flights from a similar fourteenfold

increase. General aviation, aircraft other than public passenger and cargo

carriers, is expected to grow fourfold, reaching 20,800 flights per month in

the Boston area by 1990. Logan's present total of 15,000 commercial passenger

flights per month is expected to swell to 18,200 by 1990. As with cargo flights,

this total would be far greater were it not for new aircraft of greater capacity.

Discrete time-passenger demand projections have been made for Boston

by both the M.P.A. and Lockheed. As Figure 4.5 shows, our time curve

predictions concur well with both of these sets of projections.

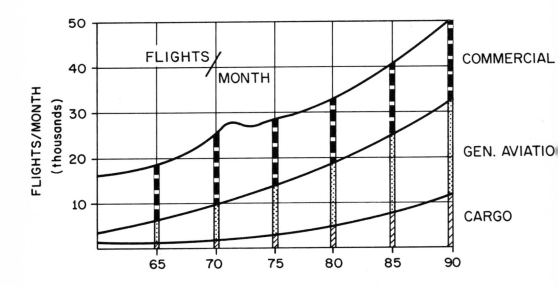

Figure 4.4 Future Demand for Service by Category

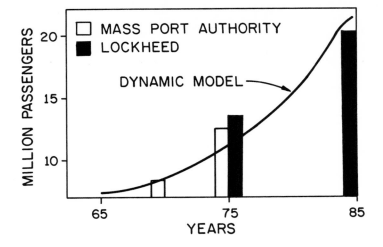

Figure 4.5 Service Demand Predictions Compared

Demand studies have revealed the major fact that short-haul trips primarily account for Boston's air traffic. In exploring passenger service demand, we investigated the origin and destination patterns for flights using Logan. We likewise projected the demand for future destinations. 74% of Logan flights will link Boston and other major East Coast cities. Of the total air traffic, the air shuttle service between Boston and New York will account for 54% of all flights; those to and from Philadelphia and Washington will constitute another 19%. The computer foresaw little alteration in the percentage situation in the future. Boston's high percentage of short-haul traffic is an important factor in planning for future airport service in the area since, as has been mentioned in this chapter, there are basic differences in the characteristics of short and long-haul air transportation.

## 4.6    V/STOL Airport Site Selection

In previous sections we have explored the many-faceted problem of designing future air and sea terminals for Boston. The facilities we propose should provide the best service possible while minimally disrupting the community they serve; they should afford financial success without generating adverse side effects.

We will recall that in the realm of air demand, prominent sources predict that through 1990 short-haul trips will monopolize, as they do presently, three quarters of service. Given the brevity of these numerous trips, convenient service will dominate user considerations. A major portion of the airport system, then, should consist of local short-haul terminals dispatching planes to prime destinations.

We have already presented formidable arguments which favor V/STOL short-haul transportation between the Northeast's cities. These smaller, lighter aircraft will capitalize upon the vertical nature of modern cities: stacked modular terminals will hold passenger and baggage services; roofs offer space for landing and loading; V/STOL terminals will require far less space than conventional airports. Decreased space demands and diminished noise levels will permit these terminals to fit unobtrusively into communities. In addition, when one situates terminals near suitable access routes - as in our proposed design - the additional traffic generated by terminals can be readily absorbed by the highway system. Last, V/STOL craft can operate simultaneously with fixed wing craft; general or commercial aviation does not preclude or endanger V/STOL flights.

Optimum terminal placement will be dictated by access times from major population concentrations of users and by compatibility with existing communities. In order to calculate user estimates an approximate scheme was devised. On a transparency over a map of the area were recorded "use factors": the population multiplied by the average income, which gives a rough likelihood of airport use by people in a location. This technique revealed that for the metropolitan area between Route I-495 and the immediate Logan area, almost any region along Route 128 would be a good site, as use factors were distributed throughout this region with three main centers at Quincy in the south, Newton in the west, and Salem in the north.

From further studies of the region, we conclude that three strategically place short-haul terminals can place most of greater Boston within 15 minutes of a terminal. A 15 minute trip will deter only 10% of the passenger population (the annual population which would fly if no access time were needed). One terminal should be situated in downtown Boston, one in the northern suburbs, and one in the southern suburbs.

The question of local acceptance was then considered. Working on the premise that nobody wants to be neighbors to an airport, even an airport that is relatively quiet, it was decided that location at current airports would minimize community disruptions. The present ports remodeled to handle V/STOL flights would continue to accommodate general aviation.

While one need not at this stage plan the exact location of the ports, we propose as suitable sites Logan Airport (Figure 4.6), Norwood Airport

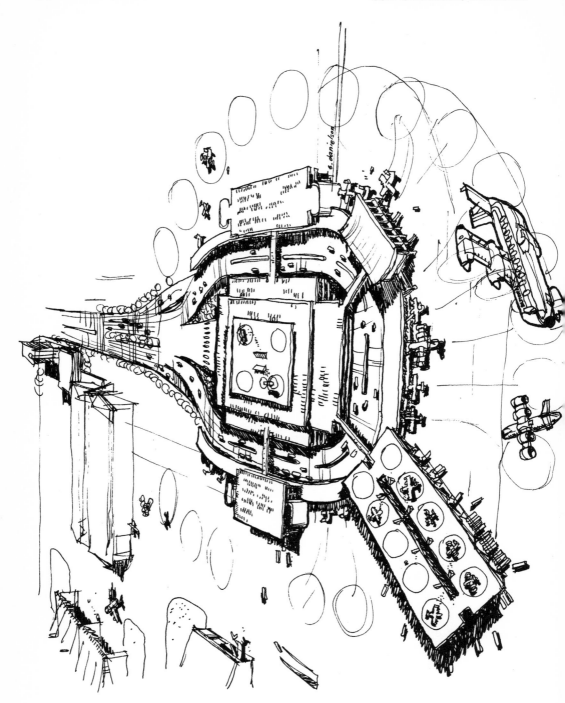

Figure 4.6 V/STOL Facilities at Logan Airport

in Norwood, and Hanscom Field in Bedford. The Logan V/STOL port would

be the downtown Boston terminal previously discussed, the latter two would

serve current demand in the Dedham area as well as the rapidly increasing

transportation requirements of the developing area north-west of Boston

in southern New Hampshire (Figure 4.7). They respectively place Lowell

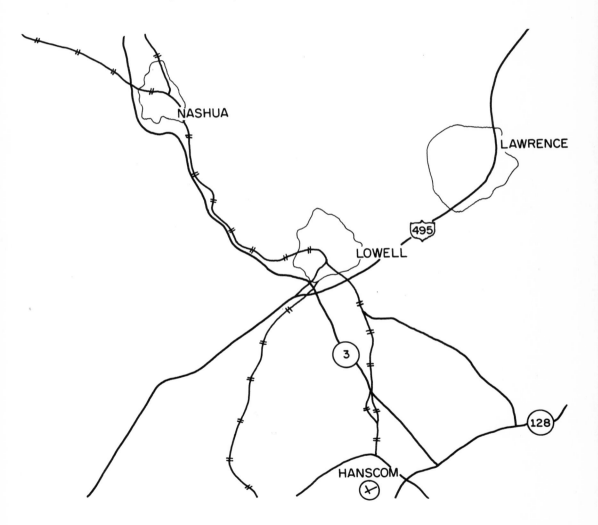

Figure 4.7  Area Served by Hanscom V/STOL Port

and Providence nearer to Boston service. This type of coverage would

equalize the market potential versus the number of terminal sites created.

If, in the future, a further outlying V/STOL port were needed, the

same criteria would recommend the vicinity of the intersection of Route

I-495 and the Massachusetts Turnpike. This location has the added

advantage of offering Worchester convenient service.

## 4.7     CTOL Port Alternatives

We have dealt thus far with Boston's short-haul airport selection.

A major fixed-wing, long-haul jetport demands a large tract of land and

a far greater investment than does a V/STOL terminal. Its land needs

as well as other operating demands impose far more deeply upon neigh-

boring communities. The grave social consequences of an improperly

placed CTOL port obliged us to consider a wide range of sites from which

to select the final jetport location.

The sites considered by our groups were the following:

1) Logan Airport, expanded

2) Brewster Islands, in Boston outer harbor

3) Duxbury, Massachusetts

4) Hanscom Field, Bedford, Mass.

5) A site in the general area of Harvard, Mass.

Its extensive present use recommends the first site. One would

be arbitrary not to weigh a location that numerous people presently

accept. The plan was to expand the present Logan facilities to whatever size would adequately handle future air transportation.

The Brewster Islands site has been frequently mentioned[9] during the past few years as a possible location for a second airport. It is a shallow area in the Outer Harbor, not presently subject to human use. The third site, a thin beach and coastal wetlands area extending into the ocean near Duxbury, Mass. suggests itself by a lack of residential use and by an isolated location at which noise will plague no one. We thought it physically the best coastal site for an airport near Boston. Hanscom Field, which was originally built as an Air Force base, is located in Bedford, Mass. near the communities of Concord, Lexington, and Lincoln. The M.P.A. presently operates it, largely for general aviation; but it is also heavily used by the military.

Finally, a tract near Harvard, Mass., an area of relatively sparse population bisected by Route I-495, we hold to be very typical of an inland site which would be built from scratch. After carefully comparing various inland sites, we chose this one as the best from the point of view of population density and area development.

Other possible sites were briefly considered and rejected. Lawrence Airport lies in a highly developed area and the North Andover region is rapidly growing. Other sites beyond Route I-495 were contemplated, but, as has been mentioned, it appears economically unwise to construct an airport further than 45 minutes from the city. The decision was based on the "spoiler effect",

---

[9] Ball, Charles H., "Airport Seven Miles Out in Harbor?", Sunday Boston Herald Traveler, Section 1, page 26, October 8, 1967.

the present convenience of Logan Airport for most users, and the proximity,

the potential competition of New York City airports.

Finally, we envisaged a floating airport system, which one could

place anywhere along the coastal waters. Although ideal in terms of many

established criteria, initial engineering estimates warn of a system cost

twice that of any of the other possibilities. Since many of the alternate

sites prove highly desirable from the viewpoint of many of our same criteria,

we reject the floating airport option.

## 4.8    CTOL Port Site

Economics served as the primary determinant in our choice of an

"optimum site" from this group of "finalists". Cost summations for airport-

seaport plans involving each of the site choices were compared, leading

to the final decision. It should be emphasized that these comparisons were

made of the whole system, as it varied with jetport alternatives, rather

than solely of jetport developments alone. The significance of this view-

point will become apparent as the discussion advances.

As mentioned above, the estimated costs at each site were

compared to a measure of the probable benefits. To justify this procedure,

we restate that anywhere within a 45 minute travel radius of the city

center, an airport attracts equal long-haul trade and passenger volume.

While nearness remains desirable, all locations promote almost equal

trade benefits. Similarly, since a major jetport operates by and large

independently of neighboring communities, peripheral benefits for any

adjacent area may be assumed rather equal in magnitude. Therefore we examine jetport location purely from the standpoint of cost.

A major factor determining the cost and acceptability of a jetport choice is the number of people who must be relocated to make way for an airport. The power of eminent domain by no means frees the state of an obligation to pay an enormous price for each house it must raze. Similarly, related problems, noise, and pollution, can be alleviated only at great expense when one deals with individual residents. One may anticipate typical per family disbursements in the order of $10,000 for outright purchase and $3,500 for noise insulation, to present some indication of the magnitude. The prospect of relocating hoards of people obviously appears extremely unattractive. Of the five sites selected, only the Harvard land presents a problem, here because of the relatively high assessed value of houses.

Surrounding areas will suffer far more; airport noise and pollution will undoubtedly produce much grief. The noise contours developed for each site are presented in Figures 4.8 and 4.9. Within the zones indicated the perceived noise level extends from 100 to 115 PNdB. Since this is already well above the level many residents find tolerable, and because of other studies, we felt anyone living within an area with a PNdB of 115 or greater should be relocated. We also identified a second zone in which people could live, but would feel serious effects and could be expected to complain vigorously. In this area, the perceived noise level is greater than 100 and less than 115 PNdB; this PNdB level would resemble that now experienced in East Boston. However, the future will see an increased

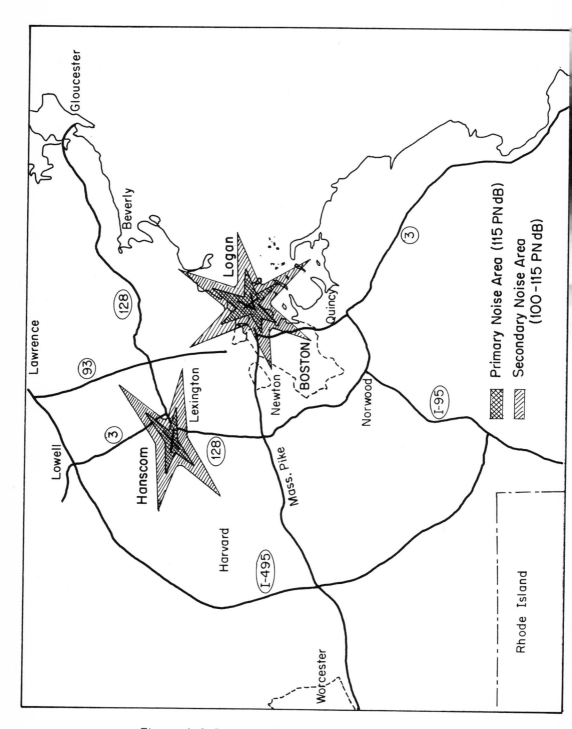

Figure 4.8  Logan and Hanscom Noise Contours

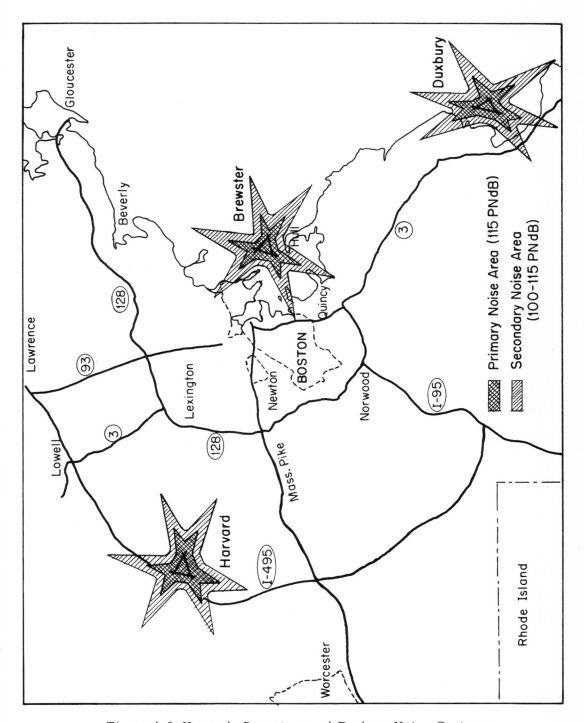

Figure 4.9 Harvard, Brewster, and Duxbury Noise Contours

problem in this range as well. The rapidly expanding number of cargo

flights will no doubt continue later and later into the night rendering the

environment in the second zone even more intolerable than at present.

Figure 4.8 charts the primary and secondary noise areas around

Logan Airport and Hanscom Field; residential use of the primary noise

area is impossible. 10,000 to 15,000 residents presently live in this

area around Hanscom and would have to be relocated. The secondary

noise area would encompass Concord, Lexington, and much of the sur-

rounding countryside. At Logan the secondary zone holds an estimated

100,000 people living in the areas of Lynn, Chelsea, and Revere. The

noise contour would also extend far into the City of Boston. Within the

area where relocation of existing residents would be essential, we

estimate that 30,000 people reside. We feel that the number of people

who must be relocated and the number of people who will seriously suffer

from aircraft noise sufficiently justify the elimination of these two

alternatives.

Figure 4.9 shows the noise contours for Brewster, Duxbury and

Harvard. Although the towns of Maynard, Stow, and Hudson lie partially

within the secondary area at Harvard and we estimate that about 10,000

people will be affected, only 3,000 to 4,000 people would have to be

actually moved at present. Duxbury is situated in a coastal wetlands

and few people live near the proposed airport site; only an estimated

300 people would have to be relocated.

After completing the noise study, we examined access time for the average user. We concluded that the average access time for a resident

of the Boston area would be approximately 40 minutes for Brewster, 45

minutes for Duxbury, and 50 minutes for Harvard. Brewster offers shorter

access time for the resident user and when a user traveling to Logan via

V/STOL wants to transfer to a long-range flight, Brewster is far superior

to the other alternatives. The traveler flying by V/STOL from a smaller

city such as Portland, Maine would land at Logan and then face a 60

minute ground trip to either Harvard or Duxbury compared with a 10 minute

trip to Brewster.

A final comparison was made of construction costs for the three

most promising alternatives. It is presented in Figure 4.10. The actual

airport construction cost was estimated at $215 million for Brewster,

$100 million for Harvard, and $150 million for Duxbury as shown on the

bargraph. We estimated the land costs as negligible at Brewster, $21.5

million at Harvard, and $2.2 million at Duxbury. New terminal facilities

could be built at a cost of $180 million at either Harvard or Duxbury, while

the Logan terminals would continue to be used in the Brewster plan. All

three alternatives included 2 V/STOL sites, of 4 pads each, at Norwood

and Bedford, costing $27 million, plus a $40 million, 10 pad, site at Logan.

The Brewster proposal would require a $17.5 million final ground link

connecting Brewster and Logan while the plan for Harvard required a $10

million ground link. The dashed line shows the expected value of the land

that would not continue to be used for airport facilities at Logan in the

future. This land could be leased or sold for other purposes, such as

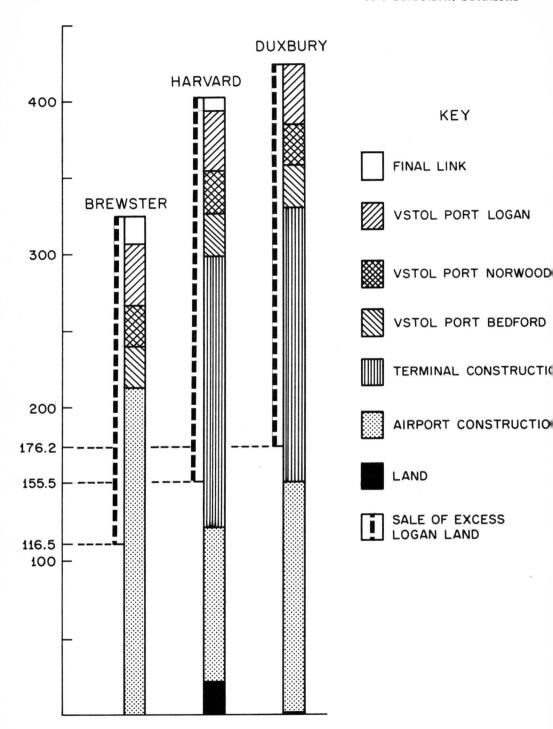

Figure 4.10  Brewster, Harvard, and Duxbury Cost Comparison

port and industrial development. For the Brewster proposal $210 million
worth of land would not be needed. The net cost of the Brewster proposal
would be the total cost of $326.5 million minus the $210 million land value
or $116.5 million. For the Harvard and Duxbury proposals $250 million
worth of land would not be needed at Logan thus giving a net cost for
Harvard of $155.5 million and for Duxbury $176.2 million.

We concluded that the Brewster site should be chosen, since it
was the best alternative in terms of noise and relocation, access time
and construction costs.

One final point remains to be made. Construction of the Brewster
runway complex would be as economical as suitable expansion at the
present Logan site. Even if one ignores the issue of relocation of East
Boston residents affected by aircraft noise, expansion at the present
Logan site continues to be as costly as construction of the Brewster runway complex. This high cost is due to the limited expansion space and
the value of land so near to downtown Boston. This equally spells affir-
mation of the Brewster site when one reintroduces the noise factor; or,
the solution to the airport noise problem effectively becomes a free bonus.

4.9     Summary and Afterthoughts

In summation then, we have considered all of the major effects
and demands of both air and sea terminals, analyzed conditions for the
particular case in Boston in depth, and developed a methodology for
terminal site selection. It should be re-emphasized that as a complement
to economic and technological considerations, social implications of

future moves were evaluated and viewed as extremely relevant.

Although comprehensive formulation of our plans will be presented
in the BOSPORUS Time Line chapter, we would like to digress for a moment
and consider several important implications of our entire plan. We have
attempted to assign a comparable dollar value to all parameters, even
those which are most qualitative, noise and pollution; yet it should be
emphasized that our intuitive appraisals have tended to coincide with
our dollar figures. Either we have rationalized to the point of attributing
unreasonably large values to social well-being, or - as we believe - the
social costs associated with a major project such as the construction of
a new port system are a significant factor. Perhaps neglect of social
aspects accounts for the failure of so many seemingly sound financial
ventures; the planners did not adequately assess social costs and weigh
them against projected economic gains.

We have recommended the outer harbor as the location for Boston's
jetport. It is wise to relate now the advantages and disadvantages from
this choice and to see how they mesh with our general selection goals.
First, we have substantially reduced the number of people who suffer
airport noise. We may, however, have precluded some social activity in
the general harbor area. The noise of the airport will not disrupt any
outdoor recreation activity; it does not preempt any other transportation
exploitation of the harbor area. To limit the amount of noise entering any
new living space built in the harbor, only sound-tight structures should
be built in residential developments. This particular option is by no means

impossible. On the contrary, any habitable structure must simply be
sound; we bar only inexpensive or temporary structures. We feel we
thereby stimulate serious planning of any future communities in the harbor
region. Deliberate designing should be pursued in any event when plans
involve a resource of such value.

A last evaluation question: is our design compatible with present
and future highway systems? Our sites for air and sea terminals have
been chosen partially on the basis of transport communication. The outlying V/STOL ports lie close to Route 128; all major Boston suburbs are
therefore within easy reach. The Logan site, although badly situated in
terms of highways, would receive users who could utilize public transport
to their principal destinations downtown. The seaport enjoys a location
central to the South East Expressway, Inner Belt, and 195 Interchange. A
short access route open only to trucking would relieve the South End of
bothersome traffic and offer shippers easy access to and from the port
facility.

Our plans are, however, based on two very important assumptions.
The first is that V/STOL aircraft will indeed compete favorably with fixed-
wing operations. The imminence of the Lockheed air bus demands that
one question this assumption. On two grounds we feel that it is reasonable. First, the added saving for city center to city center transport
should appeal distinctly to most customers. Also as airport service around
the country deteriorates, public opinion will increasingly favor V/STOL
operations and will persuade distraught decision makers. Second, with

the conclusion of the Vietnam war, the experience and technology of

helicopter research and development will be available in the field of commer-

cial transportation. Unforeseen technical advances will further enhance

the case for V/STOL.

Our second major assumption is that our design will prove poli-

tically attractive. We believe that we will pacify all antagonists to

airport expansion by controlling the adverse social characteristics of

aircraft operations in the Boston region. Further, our plan will keep cost

to a minimum and bring aircraft service closer to most users. Therefore,

we feel that every representative has positive benefits to offer his con-

stituents; government and citizens alike should therefore favor our design.

Chapter 5

THE AIRPORT

As Chapter IV has concluded, from the point of view of cost, convenience, and social benefits, location of the airport in the vicinity of the Brewster Islands is superior. Consequently, the specific design proposed here centers on this site. The design is to include whatever technological innovations will provide most efficient operation. A description of the proposed Brewster jetport and of airport constraints and concepts follows.

Chapter IV also recommended three V/STOL ports to be constructed in the Boston area. Since the particular site does little to influence V/STOL terminal design, we can without reference to preferred sites discuss general terminal facilities and functioning as envisaged by Project BOSPORUS. This discussion will follow the sections dealing with the Boston jetport.

After these descriptions of the jetport and V/STOL terminal design, we take a close look at the way in which passengers, baggage, and cargo are handled at the Logan CTOL terminal and at the V/STOL terminals. The chapter closes with a detailing of proposed access route to Logan and to Brewster.

5.1     Airport Design: Design Constraints

Aircraft landing, take-off and taxiing requirements impose several constraints on airport design and provide important guidelines. An airport must have runways of appropriate lengths, widths, and locations to accommodate the aircraft it will serve, aircraft with particular size and flight characteristics.

For any aircraft with stationary lifting surfaces, runway length is directly related to available thrusting power and the lift coefficients of the wings, and inversely related to gross weight, since the aircraft must reach a certain minimum horizontal speed (dependent on load and lift properties) in order to develop enough lift to fly. The thrust developed by the engines imparts to the plane an acceleration which is initially dependent on the plane's mass. Thus the distance a plane needs for take off (generally longer than that needed for landing) establishes runway length. This distance increases with the elevation of the airport, other factors being equal[1].

Runway width is generally related to the target area presented to a pilot on landing, and to his estimate of the available landing error buffer zone relative to the width of his plane despite slight deviations from his ideal approach path. Furthermore, for runways that are to be used under instrument flight conditions, a suitable buffer zone must be introduced to compensate for control system errors, pilot misinterpretation of signaled information, and finally for the relative sluggishness of the plane's control

---

[1] Runway Length Requirements for Airport Design, Federal Aviation Administration, 1965.

responses in relation to its forward speed.

Thus the flight characteristics of the aircraft using an airport, coupled

with flight conditions, determine the airport's runway dimensions. At present,

of the U.S. commercial transports, the DC-8 Super 63 requires the longest

take-off field length, 11,000 feet, according to the F.A.A.[2] Our design therefore

calls for runways 11,000 feet long and 150 feet wide. Newly adopted aircraft

industry resolutions state that all future aircraft will be powerful enough to take

off within the above length limit at their maximum rated payloads. Future increases

of runway width may be required, but since width dictates the general character-

istics of the airport far less than runway length, such speculation can be largely

ignored without damage to our design.

Another factor which influences an airport's general dimensions and

shape is the airport service demand, i.e., the number of flights that will

arrive and depart hourly if the airport is to meet the demand imposed by

passenger and cargo shippers. Since maintenance of safe aircraft headways

limits the capacity of a runway, an estimate of this desired number of air-

craft arrivals and departures will indicate how many runways must operate

simultaneously.

In addition to constraints provided by aircraft operations, one

natural element, the weather, dictates the runway layout and imposes

certain design features. If runways are aligned with prevailing winds both

runway length and number can be minimized; the length, since an aircraft

_____

[2] U.S. Commercial Transports, _Aviation Week_, Vol. 86, No. 10, March 6,
1967, page 205.

can take off on a shorter runway with headwinds; the number, because
disabling crosswinds will be avoided and planes will be able to use
existing runways a greater percent of the time. A record of prevailing
winds, a diagram of which is called a "wind rose", permits one to determine the number of runway orientations necessary to provide reliable
airport service[3]. The other weather conditions which influence airport
design are rain and snow. The drainage system should accommodate a
storm of such severity that it can be expected only once every five years,
and should handle a once-in-ten-years storm with only moderate damage
to runways from undrained water. Heated runways and taxiways should be
considered to eliminate snow, as airport closing in snowstorms is due
generally to unplowed runways rather than dangerous flying conditions.

The area wind rose, airport service demand, projected runway
dimensions, and the distance by which aircraft at the same altitude must
be separated to prevent intersection of flight paths establish the general
size of the airport. Configuration may change according to land availability,
but only within fairly narrow limits.

Having obtained this necessary data for Boston, we proceded to
create a specific design which would provide free and uninterrupted flow of
all commodities up to the economic-limited design capabilities of the facility,
minimizing flow restriction and smoothing the flows wherever possible.

---

[3] The F.A.A. specifies that a major airport should provide runways oriented
so that aircraft may take off or land at least 95% of the time with crosswind components not exceeding 15 mph.

## 5.2    Boston Jet Airport Design

The first step in the design of a specific Boston airport was to develop sizing requirements.  The airport is designed as a long-haul and cargo facility; our computer model predicted for cargo and long-haul service a combined peak hour demand of 72 operations per hour.  Our design will accommodate this traffic.

Current technology allows only 60 operations per hour from a runway so that two runways in each of three primary directions would be required, their orientation determined by the area wind rose (Figure 5.1).  However, advances in instrument landing systems should allow a substantial future increase in operations per hour per runway, at least to our demand figure of 72.  An advance in aircraft design may eventually permit landing with more severe cross-winds and thus possibly allow reliable operation with a single runway orientation regardless of wind conditions.  The

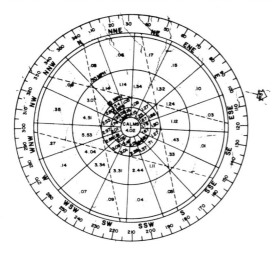

**WIND ROSE**

STATION: LOGAN INTERNATIONAL AIRPORT
PERIOD OF RECORD: JAN.,1959 -DEC.,1963
NOTE: VFR COVERAGE   15 MPH CROSS

| | |
|---|---|
| 4-22 | 77.16 % |
| 15-33 | 81.65 % |
| 9-27 | 83.51 % |
| 4-22 , 15-33 | 92.20 % |
| 15-33 , 9-27 | 94.28 % |
| 4-22 ,15-33, 9-27 | 99.60 % |

Figure 5.1 Boston Wind Rose

landing gear on the new Lockheed C5A may be turned with respect to the

airplane's axis and thus aligned with the true ground velocity vector of

the aircraft.  This combined with an advanced ILS would eliminate the

need for runways in more than one direction.  On the other hand, if aircraft

can land in 30 mph cross winds , it would be possible to use only one

runway orientation, 9-27[4], at the Brewster Island site.  This set would

have 99.3 IFR coverage and 99.36% VFR coverage.

Table 5.1 gives the principal characteristics of aircraft which can

be expected to enter commercial service between 1970 and 1990 in so far

as they affect airport design.  The designations 1980 and 1990 indicate

the year when aircraft with the characteristics given would be expected

to become available.

| Aircraft Type | Maximum Weight Lbs. | No. Pass | Cargo Capacity Lbs. | Aircraft Length | Span | Runway Length | Turn-around Time in mins. Pass. | Cargo |
|---|---|---|---|---|---|---|---|---|
| 2707 | 675,000 | 285 | ------- | 312' | 190 | 7,300 | 30 | |
| Concord | 340,000 | 140 | ------- | 193' | 84 | 10,500 | 30 | |
| C5A | 835,000 | ? | 330,000 | 250' | 220 | 10,600 | ? | 60 |
| 747 | 750,000 | 490 | 218,500 | 230' | 195 | 10,300 | 45 | 60 |
| 747 S | 900,000 | 630 | 350,000 | 280' | 215 | 10,500 ? | 40 | 60 |
| 1980 | 1,250,000 | 1200 ? | 500,000 | 320' | 250 | 10,500 ? | 30 | 60 |
| 1990 | 2,000,000 | 1700 ? | 900,000 ? | 350' | 320 | 10,500 ? | 30 | 60 |

Table 5.1 CTOL Aircraft to Enter Use from 1970 to 1990

---

[4] A pair of numbers states a runway's orientation in terms of a 360 degree
circle whose zero point is due north.  Each number notes how many degrees
from zero each end of the runway lies.  In the case of the pair 9-27, one end
of the runway is 90 degrees clockwise from north and the other end is 270
degrees.  The final zero and the degree sign are dropped.  Since runways are
straight, the difference of the two numbers is always 18 (180 degrees).

After consideration of these various factors, it was decided to

design an airport with three runways in three primary directions: 32-14,

26-8, and 20-2, as illustrated in Figure 5.2. Each Brewster runway orien-

tation deviates slightly from its Logan counterpart because we found that

with a small shift flight paths would be moved so that fewer citizens

would be afflicated by noise. As stated in section 5.1, each runway will

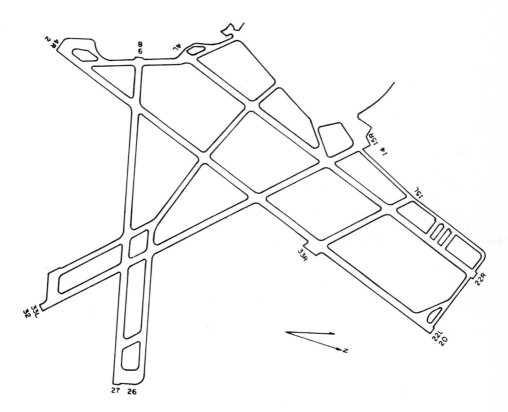

Figure 5.2 Brewster Runways

be 11,000 feet long and 150 feet wide.

The next decision concerned the number and size of gates required

for servicing aircraft. Using equation 1, we may determine the number of gates required to accommodate the peak demands.

$$\frac{\dfrac{\text{Ops./Hr.}}{60}}{\text{Gate Time (minutes)}} \times 2 = \text{Gates Required} \tag{1}$$

By using the projected gate times of Figure 5.3 we may plot the number of

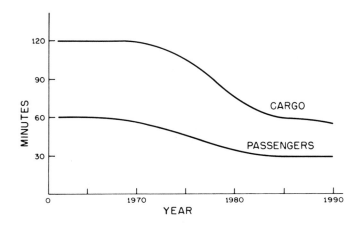

Figure 5.3 Projected Gate Times

gates required against the year. This yields a total of 36 gates in 1990,

thirty for cargo and six for passengers as is indicated in Figure 5.4.

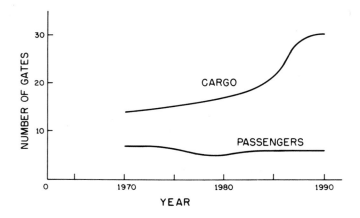

Figure 5.4 Gates Required (1970 to 1990)

The gates have been sized to accept the largest projected aircraft (Table 5.1).

Since nose-in parking will be required for the large cargo transports, this parking scheme has been adopted for all aircraft. Large turntables, as illustrated in Figure 5.5, 300 feet in diameter and floated on water, turn the aircraft after loading is complete. The turntables are rotated by electrically driven winches and the cost of turning is about two dollars per operation.

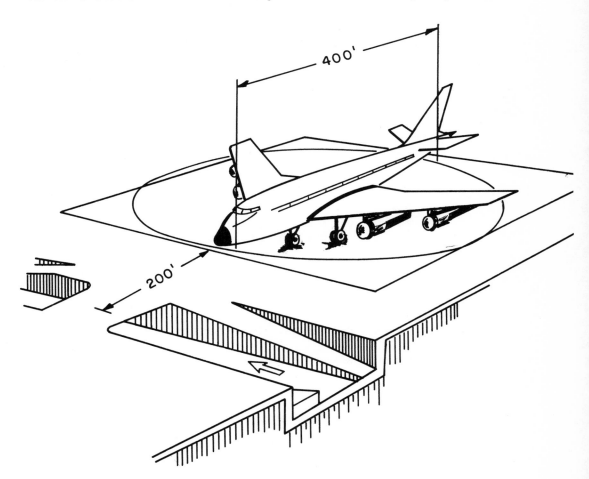

Figure 5.5 Brewster Turntables

Figure 5.6 represents the airport core layout, the circles illustrating 400 ft. gate positions. Access to the gates is by a sunken roadway three

Figure 5.6 The Airport Core Layout

lanes wide with one-way circulation. The center lane is for through traffic with the two side lanes reserved for cargo unloading or vehicle ramps, as seen in Figure 5.5. We propose that most aircraft servicing be done at the gates, but that sufficient room be allowed for twelve hangar bays.

The costs of the proposed runway system are shown in Figure 5.7. The cost of land fill will vary with the particular site. At the Brewster site, the runway sysem is constructed on fill some of which may be dredged

from the Harbor. However, further investigation may prove that material

from the Harbor area is unsuitable and that sand must be barged in from

Plymouth or some other central location.

| | |
|---|---|
| Fill & Facing | $110 Million |
| Pavements | $ 30 Million |
| Lighting, Instrumentation, Hangars, Fuel Storage, etc. | $ 40 Million |
| | $180 Million |
| Engineering & Contingencies | $ 35 Million |
| Total Cost | $215 Million |

Figure 5.7  Brewster Runway Costs

In sections 5.3 and 5.4 we briefly discuss two other airport

concepts: a floating airport and the feasibility of a circular runway.

We believed that these also were less viable than our more conventional

final design choice.

## 5.3    Floating Airport Concept

One possible design which would capitalize upon the natural

properties of the Brewster Island site is a completely floating airport,

anchored, and joined to land by a flexible transportation link (Figure 5.8).

The preliminary design of such an airport was undertaken and the results

hold promise for the future.

One feature which recommends the floating airport is the greater

use it will enjoy. Increased usefulness results from the flexibility of

reorienting the runways as necessitated by significant changes in determin-

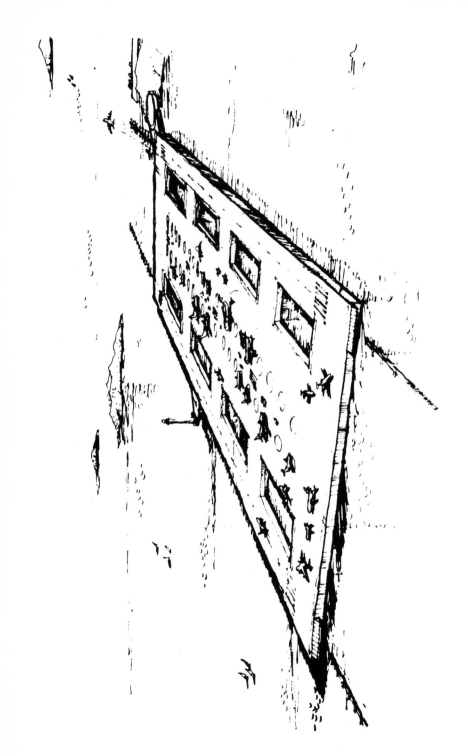

Figure 5.8 Floating Airport Concept

ing conditions, such as the prevailing winds.

The entire system as envisaged would be approximately 12,000 feet

long, 1,800 feet wide, and would weigh approximately 16 billion pounds.

Assuming that the mass is evenly distributed over the entire length, we

obtain a moment of inertia about one endpoint of $80 \times 10^{16}$ foot pounds.

The power required to rotate this structure can be computed from a knowledge

of the drag on the structure and the speed at which it is rotated.  The drag on

a body of area A, moving at velocity, v, through a fluid is given by the

formula

$$d_f = \frac{A c_d \rho v^2}{2} \tag{1}$$

where

$\quad$ A = frontal area

$\quad$ $c_d$ = coefficient of drag

$\quad$ $\rho$ $\;$ = density of the fluid

$\quad$ v = linear velocity

However, for rotary motion

$$v^2 = r^2 \omega^2 \tag{2}$$

$\quad$ r = distance from pivot point

$\quad$ $\omega$ = angular velocity

Therefore, the moment due to fluid drag on the structure as it is

rotated may be obtained by substituting into (1) for A and $v^2$ and integrating

the product of drag and the distance, r, from the pivot point along the length of the structure. With the assumptions that the depth of the structure

below the water line is 20 feet, the structure is 12,000 feet long, $c_d$ is

unity, and $\rho$ is taken as 2 slugs/ft$^3$, the resulting expression for the rotation-

al resistance due to fluid drag becomes

$$M_f = 20 \int_0^{12,000} r^3 \,^2\, dr = \omega^2 \times 10 \times 10^{16} \qquad (3)$$

While it is not proposed that aircraft be used to provide the thrust

for turning, calculation of the time required to rotate the structure through an

angle of one radian, if the take-off thrust of two Boeing 747's were exerted

at the outer end of the runway, gives an indication of the magnitudes involved.

Here the thrust would be 320,000 pounds, and the active moment approximately

$4 \times 10^9$ foot pounds. This yields a steady state turning rate, $\omega_{ss}$, of 0.012

rad./min. An approximate time constant can be computed by dividing the

moment of inertia by the fluid resistance at steady state velocity. The result

is approximately 16 minutes. The time required at constant acceleration to

bring this inertia to the steady state velocity in the absence of fluid drag

is approximately 50 minutes, with the torque indicated. Therefore, the time

required to turn the runway through one radian is longer than the 83 minutes

given by the reciprocal of $\omega_{ss}$. The energy expended in this operation is

$4 \times 10^9$ foot pounds or 1510 kw hrs.

Of the three runway orientations used at Logan, the 9-27 runway

experiences greatest use so it was chosen as the primary direction of a

floating airport. According to the windrose, the crosswind would exceed

15 m.p.h. only 16.5% of the time for such an orientation. Turning through

a full quarter rotation would require approximately two hours and would be done primarily to follow long term changes in wind direction.

The floating airport deck was designed using conventional concrete bridge design procedures. The deck is 12" thick with 12" by 54" cross beams every 7.5 feet and 18" thick stringer walls 15 feet on centers perpendicular to the cross beams. There is a garage deck, 12" thick with a 15 foot overhead clearance below the runway deck itself. This section of units is referred to as the superstructure and is supported above the barge sections by reinforced concrete columns. The barge portion is of cellular construction and operates while almost completely submerged.

The runways themselves, as well as all sections of the structure which must bear aircraft loads were designed using standard bridge design techniques which prescribed a runway deck with a thickness of 12" and 4.5 by 1.5 foot cross beams supporting it on 6 foot centers. The clear distance between supports for the cross beams is 15 feet in width and the supports (referred to here as stringer walls) are 18" thick. A floor is installed with a clear overhead of 15 feet below the cross beams and is of sufficient strength to take H16-S20 truck loads.

The over-all cost of the superstructure is $32/sq. ft. with a total area of 22 million sq. ft. giving a cost of $704 million. The floating understructure described costs $20.50/sq. ft. and has a total area of 22 million sq. ft. Addition of these two costs gives a total cost for the structure of about $1150 million.

The floating airport concept was rejected primarily because of this extravagant cost. The difficulties of adapting a single runway to various

wind conditions may also prove operationally unacceptable.

5.4     Circular Runway Concept

The feasibility of a circular runway was also explored but the

following constraints appear to bar implementation of the concept at present:

1. Pilots use the horizon for landing and don't like the idea of

landing in a confined circle. This objection may be overcome

in time by pilot education and technological advances in auto-

matic landing and take-off procedures which seem likely by

2000 A.D.

2. In aborting landing, an aircraft will sometimes, because of

crosswinds or other factors, fly over the area immediately adja-

cent to the runway at a very low altitude, maybe only two or

three feet. A banked circular runway would present a safety

hazard in this respect.

3. In landing or take-off, a tire blow-out or engine failure may

cause the aircraft to veer sharply to the right or left. For safety

there should be clear, level areas on each side of the runway.

A banked circular runway presents a hazard in this respect.

4. Though not conclusive, it is doubtful that one circular run-

way of reasonable size could handle as much traffic as a straight

runway. With straight runways one aircraft may go to the take-off

position on the end of the runway as soon as another plane has started its roll for take-off. This would not be feasible with a circular runway as the aircraft taking off might require a complete circle to gain speed for take-off or even if not required may still have to make a complete circle if aborting a take-off at high speed.

In landings, aircraft may not be spaced as close together during approach to a circular runway as to a straight runway because of the danger of the first aircraft landing making a complete circle. Also with one plane landing and one taking off, the plane taking off from a straight runway can go to the take-off spot as soon as the plane landing has made its touch-down and started its roll-out. On a circular runway the departing plane cannot go to the take-off spot until the landing plane has made its complete roll-out. Some of these problems may be overcome by making the circular runway so large in circumference that no plane under any circumstances in landing or take-off would interfere with the spotting of another aircraft on the runway for take-off or the touch-down point of another landing aircraft. A runway of this size would have to be evaluated from an area requirements and cost standpoint.

5. Icing or wet runways could cause a greater problem on a circular than on a straight runway.

Due to the above constraints, this concept does not meet pilot approval as it appears very hazardous should a plane fail to land or take off normally. In addition, the circular runway appears unable to handle as many

flights per hour under safe conditions as the straight runway. We therefore

rejected this concept in its present stage.

## 5.5    VTOL Terminal

Service from the jetport will be augmented by short-haul flights

operating from several VTOL ports. The assumption made here is that suitable

VTOL craft will be available by the mid 1970's. If developments progress in

the direction of STOL rather than VTOL aircraft, the design of the satellite

airports must reflect the need to provide short runways rather than merely

landing pads. The access, passenger, and baggage handling requirements

would be essentially the same for either.

## 5.5.1  Modular Concept

As the basis for a design that would meet all the VTOL terminal

requirements of access, demand, and future expansion, a modular unit was

proposed. Each module would include one landing pad and all essential

terminal services. All modules would be identical and as nearly autonomous

as possible in order that construction becomes a single iterative process

and expansion requires no renovation of previous construction and little

disruption of normal services.

For the proposed module, functions are assigned by floor and remain

consistent from unit to unit, creating in effect a continuous system. Although

varying traffic demands and the existence or absence of rapid-transit facilities

will influence specific designs, a six-floor model will be described as representing a typical facility.

## 5.5.2  Design Description

One end of a typical VTOL port is shown in Figure 5.9.  The first

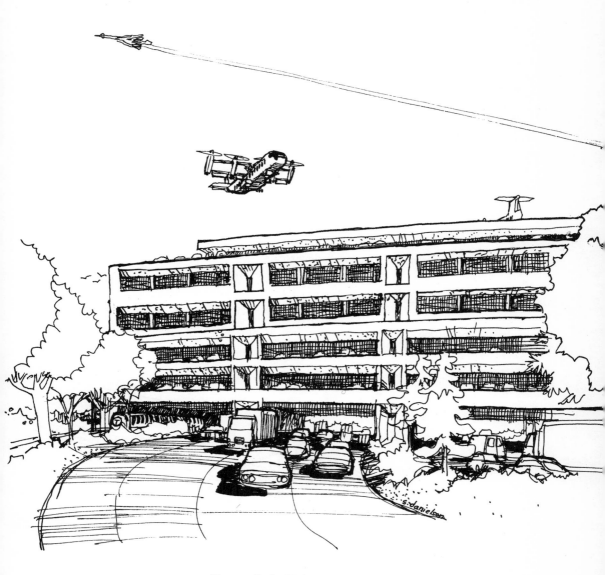

Figure 5.9  VTOL Port

or lowest floor of each module is designed so that it can straddle a previously existing roadway, divided highway, or railroad right-of-way. The second and third floors comprise a parking garage with associated baggage drop-off and claim posts and escalators. The mezzanine floor, just above the uppermost parking level, serves as the main concourse and the center of passenger activity. Here, passengers, so requiring, are ticketed, personal services are rendered, airline information centers are available, and rapid-transit loading and unloading stations are located. The last enclosed level of the module houses baggage handling machinery, heating and air conditioning equipment, and other physical plant facilities, and serves as a sound buffer or attenuation layer between the flight deck above and the busy mezzanine below. A centrally located tower serves as the single flight control center for all aircraft operations.

### 5.5.3   Gound Floor

Figure 5.10 shows the vehicular entrance to the gound floor of the

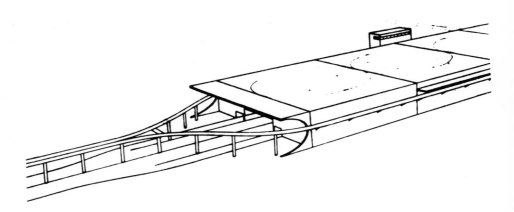

Figure 5.10 VTOL Port Ground Floor

VTOL module, a level contructed integrally with the highway. This system

provides rapid transfer of passengers from taxis, private cars, and busses

at any of a series of angular "drop-off zones", fed from the rightmost inter-

nal traffic lane. Cars can also enter from the left hand internal traffic

lanes and follow ramps leading from this level to upper level parking areas.

The ground floor drop-off area pictured in Figure 5.11 provides for

a conservative maximum of 38 motor vehicles in one VTOL module, including

4 to 6 busses on each of 3 bus drop-off zones. Each passenger car drop-off

would service 6 vehicles simultaneously, and spacing of the islands could

easily be changed in response to traffic flow predictions. In the figure,

the small numbers on the islands indicate vehicle capacity; the shaded areas correspond to information centers, conventional "Red Cap" services, personnel offices, etc.

Persons disembarking onto the curb-height safety islands proceed to the periphery of the module no more than 60 feet distant where escalators, elevators, or moving walkways carry them

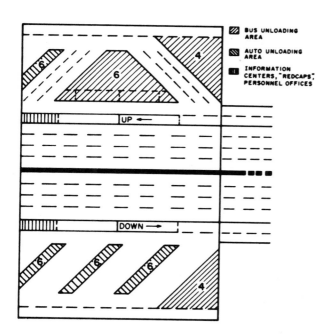

BUS UNLOADING AREA

AUTO UNLOADING AREA

INFORMATION CENTERS, "REDCAPS", PERSONNEL OFFICES

Figure 5.11 Ground Floor Drop-Off Area

to the upper level. T.V. monitors located at convenient intervals would display current flight information, pad designations, etc.

In the event that the VTOL unit not be built over a highway, the drop-off zone could easily be extended to cover the entire lower floor area and a subsidiary walkway provided to the module periphery.

## 5.5.4  Second and Third Floor

In each module the two "parking garage" floors are virtually identical, save for the two centermost modules which include floor to floor ramps. Module 2A in  Figure 5.12 is an identical mirror image of 2B as shown.  The shaded areas in the figure house baggage handling facilities: either conveyors, dumb waiters, or other types.  The small numbers indicate numbers of vehicles in each parking zone.  The spacing of vehicles within each module gives a conservative estimate of 96 vehicles for the central module, 2C, and 168 vehicles for each of the outlying modules, 2A and 2B. Primary parking is at 90 degrees to the baggage areas, but capacity may be increased by utilizing some of the unused space for parallel parking and 30 degree angle parking of a few more cars.

Slope on ramps is a gentle 7:1 and the minimum turning radius is about 35 feet.  The curved portions of the ramps are not sloped, but walled-in to insure proper heading of entering vehicles. An additional 42 vehicles per module may be obtained if this curved section is eliminated; traffic flow then relies only upon high-visibility signs.

Cost for a parking area of this type averages $12/ft^2$, totalling $0.7

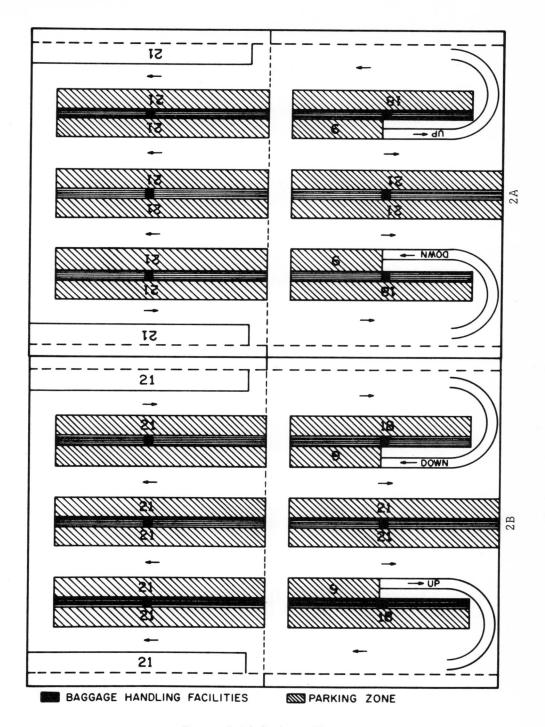

BAGGAGE HANDLING FACILITIES        PARKING ZONE

Figure 5.12 Parking Floors

million per module per floor. With the assumption that fees of $3. per day

will be collected each day for each of the 144 spaces average per floor and

that 20% of the income will cover maintenance and operation of the parking

facility, about $125,000 per year will be generated by each floor to pay

interest and amortize the debt. On the assumption of a 7% interest rate,

the facility, on this basis, would amortize itself in a little over six years.

5.5.5  Mezzanine Floor

    The center of passenger activity takes place on the spacious mezzanine

floor of the VTOL module shown schematically in Figure 5.13. Here, passengers
disembark from rapid transit vehicles or arrive by escalator or elevator from the lower level parking and limousine facilities. In the center of each mezzanine module await two "lounges" that immediately prior to take-off are elevated hydraulically and carry the passengers up through the remaining floors to board the VTOL craft. In the future, the lounge itself, complete with luggage containers, might be

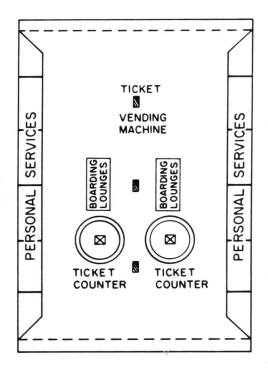

Figure 5.13  Mezzanine Floor

made a part of the aircraft and be loaded as a unit. With this plan, provision would be made for storage and handling of sufficient container-lounges to permit designating one for each flight for which passengers would be expected to be checked in.

For the convenience of passengers not previously ticketed, conventional counters would be provided. Ticket vending machines activated by credit cards would also be located at convenient intervals on the mezzanine floor. Rent-a-car booths and personal services would be available along the sides of the module and carousel-type units might deliver baggage to incoming passengers.

## 5.5.6  Handling Floor

Serving both as a noise attenuation layer and the physical plant center, the handling floor would house passenger elevator equipment, the central baggage handling system facility equipment, consisting of elevators, conveyor belts, and baggage return ducts, as well as heating and air conditioning equipment. Storage and claim areas for unmarked or unclaimed baggage also would be provided in each module.

## 5.5.7  Flight Deck

The uppermost level of each VTOL module would serve as the flight deck which would measure 200 by 200 feet with 50 foot extension aprons constructed on the endmost pads to provide adequate "ground" visibility for pilots during take-off or landing. Flush-mounted bay doors for lifting lounges and refueling lines, and landing lights would be the only "obstructions"

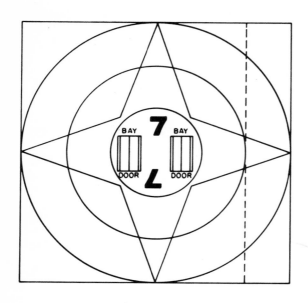

Figure 5.14 Flight Deck

on the pad surface. A retaining fence might be added along the entire perimeter of the flight deck to serve as a noise buffer, a safety measure in case of an abort caused by gusting winds, and a protection for workmen or others who might have occasion to walk around the flight deck area. VTOL craft would be serviced at nearby ground level pads. A schematization of the flight deck is shown in Figure 5.14.

## 5.6    Passenger, Baggage, and Cargo Handling

The efficient operation of any airport requires that facilities be provided for the fast, comfortable, and convenient transfer of passengers and their baggage between the point at which they leave another transport mode and enter the aircraft or vice versa. Both passengers and cargo must transfer as they progress through their trip; efficient means for making such transfers must be provided for in order to eliminate unnecessary effort or delay.

The passenger should not have to walk long distances to reach his plane, and he should not have to stand in line to get a ticket or to claim his baggage. Similarly, cargo should not have to be loaded into a truck to travel to the airport, then reloaded into a cargo pod which is finally loaded into the plane.

In the following sections, two alternate schemes are proposed for improving the movement of passengers, baggage, and cargo through long-haul jet terminals. The first is intended for implementation as quickly and as cheaply as possible and thus relies on state-of-the-art methods; the second is intended for long-range planning, and is designed for maximum effect, unhampered by the necessity to conform to current practices. Following this discussion, several possible handling schemes appropriate for use with V/STOL systems are described.

In all cases, the goal is a smooth, quick flow of goods and people, and it is in this interest that conflict between streams of passengers and cargo is eliminated. By maintaining user and commodity flows on noninter-secting trajectories, by eliminating flow obstacles and bottlenecks, and by using automatic control and locomotion in favor of their human counterparts, we have attempted to aid terminal users to achieve their desired transfers with greater ease and speed than is now available.

## 5.6.1  System I Facilities for Logan Long-haul Terminal

With the runways for the long-haul operations at the Brewster  and the VTOL facilities handling the short-haul traffic, the main Logan terminal area can be devoted to the task of processing air cargo and the long-haul passenger and his baggage, and dispatching them to the planes at Brewster.

The long-haul passenger load is expected to reach a peak of 5,000 passengers per hour during peak travel periods by 1991 with planes capable of seating 500 passengers each. It is this number of passengers and 4,000 tons per hour of cargo that the Logan terminals must handle.

The System I facilities described in the following pages can be adopted readily in that they require no change in the aircraft and no unique ground link. At the same time, this system has the advantage that the passenger walks, without baggage, only from his parked car, or from the drop-off point in front of the terminal, approximately 185 feet on one level through the terminal to an awaiting mobile lounge. Enroute he must make only one short stop at one machine. Once he enters the mobile lounge, the lounge delivers him along a scenic coastal route to his waiting aircraft, a trip of approximately 9 minutes. He boards the aircraft directly from the lounge.

Passengers will arrive at the airport by different transportation modes, some with tickets, some without, some with credit cards, some without. The following material gives a more detailed account of the exact procedure for accomodating each type of passenger.

If a passenger arrives in a car which he wishes to park he proceeds directly to the parking lot. On each floor of the parking lot are four baggage deposit and claim areas. He may drive up to these areas and deposit his bag and then park his car, or may park and carry his bag to this area, a maximum distance of 250 feet. Figure 5.15 illustrates the parking, baggage facility interplay. Focusing on the baggage deposit system, we observe that the passenger places his baggage in a fiberglass container called a "lump".

Figure 5.15  Logan System I Parking and Baggage Facility

The passenger is then issued a tag, one half of which he retains while the
other half is inserted in a special holder on the lump. This tag carries a
number and an airline identification; when the passenger puts his bags into
the lump system he need only know the airline he intends to utilize. The
passenger then walks to the terminal area and his bag is sent to the baggage
storage area in the terminal.

The passenger who arrives by public transportation or who wishes
to be let off at the front door of the terminal finds a similar baggage check
point conveniently located. Once again he is relieved of all baggage handling
until he arrives at his destination.

The departing passenger enters an elevator or takes an escalator from
the parking area to the upper level of a two-story building. If the passenger
already has his ticket he goes to a "check-in processor" and inserts his ticket
and lump tag. The machine logs the passenger in on his flight and tells the
lump system to forward his baggage from storage to the area where airplane
baggage pods are loaded. The machine also stamps his lump tag with a number
indicating the airplane baggage subunit into which his baggage will be loaded.
This subunit number will speed retrieval of his baggage at destinations where
the lump system may not be in use. If the passenger does not have a ticket,
but has a credit card, he may insert his credit card and lump tag in the
machine, type in his flight number and receive his ticket from the machine.
If the passenger has no ticket and wishes to pay cash he goes to a ticket counter
for personal service by airline employees. Any passenger unfamiliar with the
system or so desiring may, of course, go to the counter for personal service.

The passenger then proceeds to his mobile lounge. When filled, the mobile lounge pulls away from the terminal, is lowered to the ground, and driven to Brewster. The lounge, reaching the plane, drives up beside it, raises level to the plane door, with some final maneuvering and the extension of a short ramp, the doors of the lounge open and the passenger walks onto the plane. Figure 5.16 portrays these operations.

Incoming passengers leave the plane for the lounge, are driven back to Logan, and exit from the lounge on the lower floor of the terminal. Baggage subunits from the plane have been parked on the lower floor baggage claim area and the passenger retrieves his bag from the appropriate subunit. The passenger can then carry his bag to his car or can put his bag into the lump system and proceed to his car without baggage. At the closest baggage deposit and claim area he inserts his lump tag in a baggage claim slot and his baggage is delivered to him in approximately 60 seconds. The movement of the bag from the airplane baggage subunit by the passenger is only required until such time as incoming baggage can be sorted into lumps which can be fed automatically into the system. Once terminals at other cities install the complete lump system, the passenger can disembark from the mobile lounge, walk directly to the baggage claim area nearest his car, insert his tag and have his bag delivered.

All terminals are to have two levels with access roads at each level. All departing passengers are processed on the second floor and all incoming passengers are processed on the ground floor. Thus complete separation between the two is preserved. An incoming or departing passenger passes through but one level. Transit passengers, who are both incoming and departing passengers,

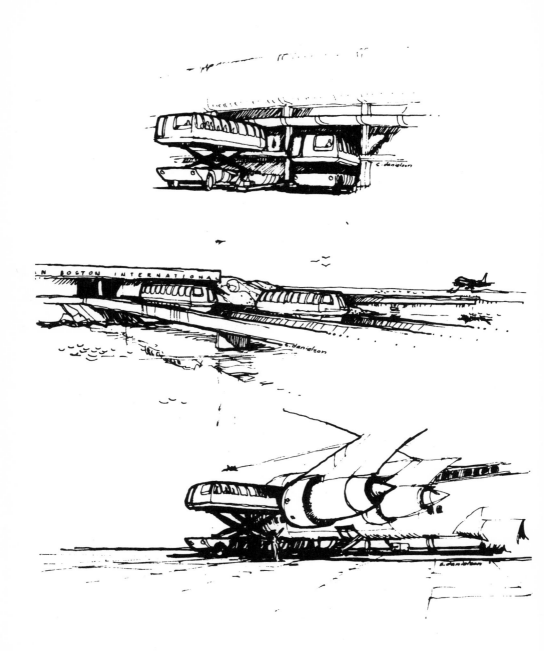

Figure 5.16 Mobile Lounge

would be required to change levels.

In a typical second floor terminal layout, there are 6 lounges, each of which can seat 200 people. Each lounge will adjoin four mobile lounges (each of which seats 125) reached through 4 loading doors. The 200 seat lounge and four loading doors form a unit, used in loading one 500 passenger plane. Present studies indicate about half the departing passengers arrive at the terminal at least 15 minutes before departure time. For passengers arriving earlier than 15 minutes early, the 200 seats in one lounge are available. At 15 minutes before departure time the mobile lounges will be placed in position and the early comers and subsequent arrivals will take one of the 500 seats available. There is ample ticket counter space to handle the passengers requiring personal service, estimated at 200 people out of a flight of 500. This assumes, as indicated by present statistics, that one-half, or 250 people, have tickets and can use the check-in processor, 50 people have credit cards and will use this machine, and 200 people will procure tickets with cash, or will have credit cards and prefer personal service. Figure 5.17 diagrams the second floor terminal facility plan.

The ground floor houses the automatic baggage handling system and the interim baggage pick-up area. This interim baggage pick-up area is a space where the airplane baggage subunits are deposited and passengers may remove their luggage from them. When the lump system has been adopted by numerous cities, the interim baggage pick-up area will be replaced by facilities of the automatic baggage handling system expanded to sort baggage subunits back into lump units.

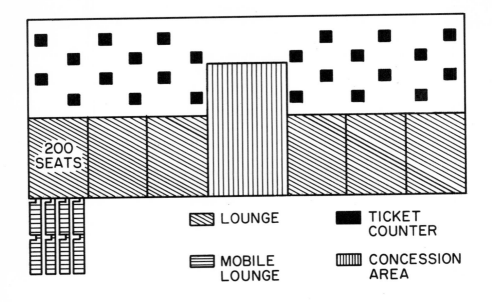

Figure 5.17 System I Second Floor

Figure 5.18 depicts the present layout and currently planned future

additions to the Logan Airport terminal complex.  Our typical terminal layout

conforms to the exterior dimensions of the Southwest terminal building.

One terminal building of this size, housing two major airlines has ample

room for each airline to process 12 aircraft of the 707 size or three 500-passenger

aircraft simultaneously, or an equivalent combination.  Each area used to load

one 500-passenger aircraft has four loading gates and a 200-seat lounge in the

terminal.  Ample room remains for concession areas.

In adapting Logan to this new terminal system, only five major steps

are required:

1) The first two floors of the present North and Southwest terminals

will have to be modified.

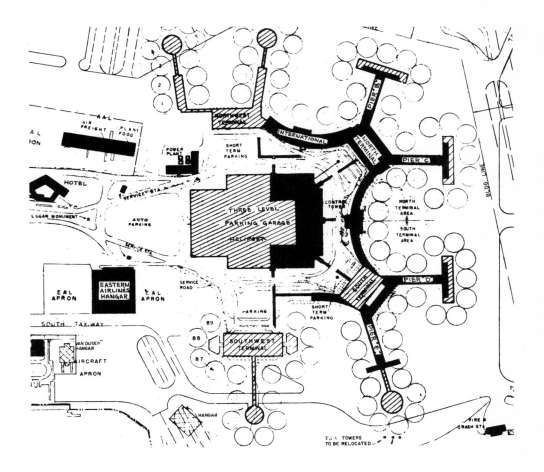

Figure 5.18 Present Logan Airport Terminal Complex

2) Two new terminals will be needed and the North terminal must

be expanded.

3) The parking garage will have to be expanded to house 10,000

cars.

4) The automatic baggage handling system (lump system) will have

to be installed.

5) Initially, 20 moible lounges will have to be constructed and
in its ultimate 1991 configuration, 120 will be required.

The four terminal buildings will be utilized as follows:

1) Southwest (Eastern) Terminal - Eastern and small domestic airlines

2) South Terminal - American and National Airlines

3) North Terminal - United, Northwest, and TWA Airlines

4) International Terminal - all international airlines

## 5.6.2   System I Facilities Detailed

The check-in processor, in conjunction with the central computer,
performs several functions:

1) Automatically dispenses tickets to credit card holders

2) Maintains a running total of number of lumps sent to each airplane baggage pod for a particular flight

3) Stamps lump tag indicating airplane pod which will deliver
baggage

4) Records tickets dispensed to credit card holders by noting credit
card numbers and totals the number of people it has ticketed for
each flight.

The check-in processor is activated by a combination of two required
inputs, a ticketing input and a baggage input. The ticket input is activated
when a passenger inserts his ticket, or inserts a credit card, and types in
his flight number and destination. In the latter case a ticket is issued to the
customer and the billing is recorded. The baggage input is activated by insertion of a lump tag or pressing the "no baggage" key. If a person has more than

one lump tag he must go to the counter for special attention. A check-in processor

behind the counter operated only by airline personnel handles ticketing and

baggage functions independently. The attendant inserts a passenger's lump

tags into this machine in turn, each time typing in the flight number and des-

tination. The system then sends those lumps to the appropriate airplane baggage

pod.

The check-in processor keeps a running total of the lumps by flight and

airplane baggage pod, knows where to direct the present lump and stamps the

lump tag with the number of the baggage pod into which a particular bag will

be loaded. A warning is displayed to the attendant before a baggage pod is

filled so that he can be sure that all the bags belonging to a single passenger

are loaded into the same pod. This pod number stamp is only necessary until

other airports accept the lump system.

The system records reservations by credit card number; upon insertion

of credit card the system recognizes this number and issues the ticket. The

system, having all reservations recorded, will sell all excess tickets avail-

able on a first come, first served basis. A small T.V. screen over the machine

informs the passenger if no seats are available on the flight he has selected

and informs him of the next appropriate flight number and departure time. The

screen can also be used to inform a customer of his own improper operation

of the machine.

The automated baggage handling system is composed of five main

elements:

1) Baggage input and claim station

2) Interconnecting moving belt system

3) Baggage transfer points

4) Baggage storage and routing area

5) Central computer system.

At each baggage depo, a person inserts his luggage into a lump capable of handling two bags and obtains a two-part lump tag which is identified by airline and tag number. (Passengers with luggage such as golf clubs or skies which would not fit into a lump must check their baggage at the counter.) The passenger places one part of the lump tag in a slot on the lump and retains the other part. He then pushes a button which directs the lump from the deposit area to the storage area in the airline terminal corresponding to the button he pushed. As the lump enters the storage area the lump tag is read by a magnetic sensing device which feeds tag number and time of entry into the system, to the computer, and directs the lump to an empty storage space. When the lump tag is inserted into the check-in processor and stamped with an airplane subunit number, the storage and routing area is directed to send the lump to the specific airplane baggage area designated. Twelve assembly areas will handle up to three 500 passenger planes with four assembly areas designated for each plane.

When a flight is ready to be loaded with baggage, the system is keyed and all bags for that flight are sent to the loading area. In the final system, lumps would by loaded automatically into the airplane baggage pod. But until an automated system is installed at a sufficient number of cities served by an airline, the bags will be removed from the lumps and loaded into the appropriate airplane baggage pods by hand.

Arriving baggage, if contained in lumps, is automatically inserted into the system, sent to the storage area. When an arriving passenger inserts his lump tag into a baggage claim slot at one of the baggage depo areas, the bag is taken from storage and sent to its destination. If the bags arrive in loose form, that is, not in lumps, the airplane baggage pods are positioned on the terminal ground floor where passengers retrieve their bags from one of the four baggage areas and either carry their bags to their car or insert their bag in a baggage deposit and claim area, located on the ground floor of the terminal, go to their car and by insertion of their lump tag in a baggage claim slot have their bags automatically delivered to them.

Every 24 hours the system prints out the lump tag number of all lumps that have been in the system for more than 24 hours. These bags, if desired, can be called for in the lost and found area which will be located in dead storage. This keeps the system from becoming saturated with abandoned bags.

Figure 5.19 is a diagram of the system's information flow. The automatic storage area is comparable to that found in fully automated warehouses.

The mobile lounges will handle 62 people seated. The lounges are 10 feet wide and 40 feet long and can attain a speed of 60 m.p.h. in the lowered position. Four hydraulic lifts can raise a lounge to reach a plane door 21 feet high. The lounges are identical at both ends to keep the operator from having to back away from the plane into the mobile lounge roadway. The lounges can be mated so as to load or off-load in tandem. In this fashion 8 mobile lounges can load through any combination of plane or terminal doors

from 1 to 8. Normally 4 terminal gates and plane doors would be used for one
500 passenger plane.

It is presently estimated that cleaning of the large capacity planes
will require 41 minutes at one stop. As the mobile lounge can make the trip
from Logan to Brewster in about 9 minutes, plane cleaning time rather than
the mobile lounge transit time required to make the round trip will be the limiting
factor. When, and if, the cleaning time is reduced below 10 minutes, different
lounges can be used for enplaning and deplaning passengers.

Baggage will be moved by conventional prime movers towing either one
or two 40-foot long trailers each carrying 18 airplane baggage pods. The trailers

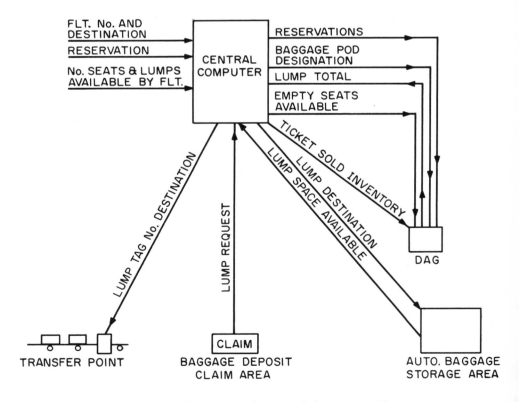

Figure 5.19 Baggage System Information Flow

which can be hydraulically raised or lowered to match baggage loading doors
on the plane, are positioned next to the plane and the baggage pods rolled
off onto the plane. A large capacity plane may hold 35 baggage pods.

Air freight arriving at Logan is all delivered to the cargo warehouses
where it is sorted and loaded into standard cargo containers. These containers
are delivered to plane-side at Brewster on the same trailers that handle passenger baggage.

The costs estimated for upgrading Logan in accordance with the above
described system are as follows:

| | | |
|---|---|---|
| 1) Expand one terminal and build two additional ones | $10.0 M |
| 2) Renovate two existing terminals | 3.3 M |
| 3) Add to parking garage | 17.6 M |
| 4) Add second level roadway structure | 9.0 M |
| 5) Install automated baggage system | 6.5 M |
| 6) Purchase mobile lounges | 3.0 M |
| 7) Purchase baggage and cargo trailers | 1.5 M |
| 8) Purchase prime movers | .5 M |
| | Total | $51.4 M |

A moving sidewalk will probably be required also. Its cost is estimated
at $4 million, thus bringing the total to $55.4 million.

In summary, System I offers a number of clear advantages. Baggage
carrying is eliminated and the passenger need pass through only one terminal
area on one level. Ticketing and baggage checking are separated, saving time
and speeding ticket counter transactions. A passenger need not go to the

ticket counter at all unless he wishes to buy his ticket for cash or has a unique

problem since automatic machines dispense and process tickets. Baggage

checking and retrieval is also automated. These quicker services allow the

passenger to arrive closer to the departure time for his plane and permits the

airlines to handle as many as three 500-passenger planes at once with speed

and efficiency.

5.6.3  System II

The System II design proposal is an integration of Project METRAN[5]

with a future air transportation system design. If it is taken as a basic premise

that a major trouble lies within the airport itself, a significantly better way of

handling passengers and baggage must, in the long run, be found.

The METRAN report[6] proposes use of a dual-mode vehicle, known as

the BOS vehicle. This consists of a chassis which carries removable standard-

size pods. The pods may hold either passengers or cargo. The pods including

their contents may be transferred with their contents easily and quickly from

one mode of transit to another. Handling a standard size pod, no matter what

it contains, is cheaper and quicker than transferring people and baggage from

one vehicle to another or carrying odd-sized cargo lots from one vehicle to

another. The BOS vehicle as proposed in the METRAN report would be the basic

ground transportation vehicle for passenger and cargo handling at the air terminal

---

[5] Project METRAN is a high speed, dual mode ground transportation system
   designed at M.I.T. in the spring of 1966 as a possible solution to the ground
   transportation ills which currently plague travelers.
[6] Project METRAN, M.I.T. Report No. 8 , M.I.T. Press, 1967.

METRAN is a system which relies on automated guidance of high speed vehicles to make ground transportation quicker and more convenient for passengers and cargo forwarders. A network of guideways, replacing highways and streets as they now exist, carries all vehicles at high speeds and under automatic control without passenger steering or control. Within metropolitan areas such guideways will eliminate traffic congestion, and in outlying areas point-to-point travel times can be greatly reduced. The METRAN system as proposed for Boston could easily include a guideway link from Logan Airport to the runway complex at the Brewsters. This link would be restricted to airport passenger transportation and cargo vehicles.

A typical journey utilizing this system might be as follows. A businessman living in Newton wishes to fly to Los Angeles. After calling the airport to learn the flight time and reserve a seat he gets into his dual model automobile in his garage and drives to the nearest entrance to the automated guideway. His car is given a rapid automatic safety check and is cleared for use on the high-speed lane. He indicates Logan as his destination by dialing a number code into the on-board control unit, and relaxes with his newspaper for the brief trip. The trip from Newton to Logan takes approximately 15 minutes.

At Logan the car is directed into a grid of drop-off platforms where the passenger gets out and removes his bags. He had dialed the number for the airport parking garage just before getting out, and now when he closes and locks his door, his car is taken automatically to the garage to be stored until he summons it on his return. An escalator carries him to the concourse floor. There the passenger finds the platform number for his flight to Los

Angeles, and takes the appropriate escalator down to the pod area. Here he

sees rows and rows of pods being boarded, and overhead cranes loading the

filled pods onto BOS vehicles for the ride out to the Brewster runway complex.

Having loaded his luggage into the baggage drawer of the first pod with an

empty seat, he gives his name to the hostess standing at the door, and boards

the pod. The thirty seats inside, with three, four, and three seats abreast

all face the long side of the pod. When the pod is full, the sliding doors are

closed and the crane transfers the pod to a waiting BOS vehicle. The trip out

to the Brewsters takes approximately four minutes, and there the pod is loaded

into the plane. As soon as the pod is in position inside the plane, the sliding

doors at each end open and the pod is joined to the rest of the pods and a

restroom and galley pod. With all the pods aboard, the flight is ready to

take off. Once airborne, the hostess will come around to take the passengers'

money or credit cards, and bring drinks, and serve them meals.

If the passenger has a car of his own, as in the example above, he

may drive to the airport. If he intends to leave his car in the automated parking

garage, no one will have to drive him to the airport. He will not have to walk

from the parking garage into the terminal building, since his car will be handled

automatically once he leaves it. The passenger platforms in the grid area

(which replaces the present drop-off zones) have machines which can read

a card identifying the driver as the proper user of the car. This card might

be the car's registration card, or a plastic card with the license plate dupli-

cated on it. No matter what the system used, it is possible to provide unique

identification for every driver and car. By inserting this card in a reader,

the returned passenger summons the car from the garage to the grid area.
It will be delivered to the nearest empty platform space or even, with some
additional control complexity, to the platform from which the summons was
delivered. If the passenger wants to drive to the airport, but doesn't want
to leave the car in the garage, he will probably have to be accompanied
since the guideway may not extend all the way back to his house. In most
cases the guideway will not carry local traffic, but rather will serve residential areas by frequent access ramps.

If the passenger has no car of his own or does not wish to use it,
he may summon a taxi or ride a bus to the airport, just as at present. However,
because there will be no traffic congestion, the traveler need not allow as
large a safety margin of time for the trip as he does now.

The possibility of sending pods to collect passengers at their point
of origin was considered and rejected as unfeasible. The pods will hold 30
passengers, and in most cases these 30 people will come from widely scattered
points. The first passenger to get into the pod would then have to ride with it
as it picked up others, and all requests for at-home pick-up would have to
be carefully scheduled and regulated to insure that the pod arrived at the airport in time for the flight. However, pod pick-up could be provided from a
few satellite terminals in a metropolitan area. Pick-up of cargo pods appears
more certainly efficient. In many cases the forwarder will have enough cargo
to fill a pod, or multiple pods, and can have them assembled at one point at
a definite time. Forwarders who want fractional space in a pod could arrange
a sharing schedule, which would also result in single-point pick-up. The

manufacturer who uses pods frequently would be likely to have his own BOS

vehicles or to arrange with a private trucking firm with BOS vehicles to carry

his cargoes to the airport. Both cargo and passengers will be scheduled to

arrive at the airport within a relatively short time period before the flight,

since turn-around time will be lowered with the pods and we wish to minimize

pod storage at the airport. The advantages of boarding the passenger pods at

the airport outweigh the disadvantages of the extra transfer involved; but with

cargo, pod pick-up and delivery at the site of business appears most advantaged

Passengers would still be responsible for their own transportation to

the airport. If they are coming from the central business district, passengers

may also use the GENIE vehicle, a small ten-passenger bus. In downtown

business areas, where there are many businessmen who want to get to the

airport, yet not enough to justify BOS pick-up, the GENIE bus may provide

shuttle service between downtown and the airport. The passengers coming from

the suburban areas will utilize private automobiles or taxis.

All these ground vehicles will arrive at the airport on the guideway

network. A single lane of automated guideway can handle 12,000 vehicles

per hour if the vehicles move at 60 m.p.h. with 10 foot headways. Our demand

model indicates that by 1990, the passenger demand will reach 5,000 passengers

per hour during peak hours. Even if each peak hour passenger arrived in his

own car, a single lane of guideway at the airport could handle the total traffic

at less than half its capacity. To accommodate the vehicles as they slow

down near the airport, multiple guideway lanes must, of course, be provided.

Cargo flights peak later in the evening and earlier in the morning than passenger flights, so that there will be little interference on the guideway between passenger and cargo vehicles. The cargo vehicles will be directed straight to the runway complex, while passenger vehicles will be stopped at Logan for passenger transfer to the pods.

A grid of passenger drop-off platforms, as shown in Figure 5.20, is provided on the top floor of the terminal building. The cars, busses, and taxis will all use the same grid, but portions of it will be allotted to each different type of vehicle since they have different borading times. Each vehicle will stop between two platforms, allowing passengers to get out on both sides without dodging passing vehicles, as they now must in drop-off areas. If we again assume the worst possible case - that every peak hour passenger arrives in his own car - a grid to handle 5,000 cars per hour, with an average drop-off time of one minute, requires approximately 85 car slots. As shown in the sketch of the grid area, the space required is an area approximately 160 feet wide and 250 feet long. Each of the diagonal slots in the sketch is a drop-off lane, while the horizontal lanes and selected vertical lanes supply the drop-off lanes. Since there will be a steady stream of traffic in the supply lanes, for safety reasons, we don't want passengers crossing those lanes; the passengers are constrained, therefore, to move freely along any of the six horizontal rows, each of which is served by two escalator-stair combinations, but they may not cross the horizontal or vertical supply lanes.

The automated parking garage lies only a short distance from the terminal building. In fact, the present parking garage might be remodeled

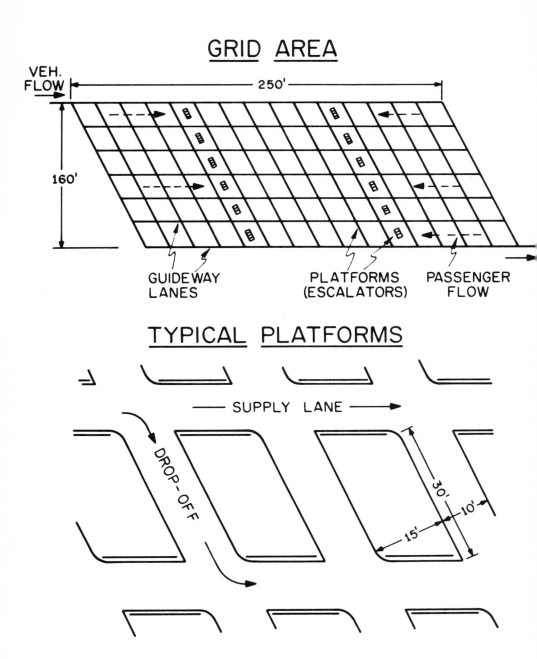

Figure 5.20 Passenger Drop-Off Grid

for automated operation. Current design practice assigns two car stalls

in a garage for each peak hour passenger. A 500-passenger peak load therefore

indicates the need for a 10,000 car garage. The parking garage proposed in

the METRAN report has a capacity of 1280 cars with a flow rate of 1800 vehicles

per hour. To accommodate 10,000 cars, the garage at the airport would have to

be nine times the size of the METRAN garage, and will be assumed to have nine

times the vehicles flow rate, or 16,200 vehicles per hour. This is more than

adequate to handle the vehicle flows expected in 1990, and it assures the

arriving passenger that he may summon his car and have it arrive within five

minutes. The extraction of summoned cars from the garage will be given

priority over the storage of cars of departing passengers.

Cargo vehicles need no transfer grid. The cargo pod is loaded on a

BOS vehicle at the forwarder's warehouse, and the vehicle delivers the pod

directly to the cargo loading area at the airport. The cargo vehicles move in

a loop through the plane loading pads with the cargo pods transferred either on

or off the pads. Some termporary storage of pods may be allowed while the

plane is being loaded, but the forwarder will not be allowed to send his pods

to the airport more than an hour or so before flight time, depending on the time

it takes to load the planes. Incoming cargo pods are met by empty BOS vehicles,

and the pods are loaded for direct shipment to the receiver. Cross transfer of

cargo is handled by shunting pods around the loop.

Cross transfer of passengers may also be handled easily with the pod

system. If there are enough passengers to justify it, an entire pod may be

filled with passengers making cross-connections at the same intermediate airport. It is more likely that transfer passengers will be in small groups

which do not justify direct use of a pod. In such cases, the passenger

walks from one pod to another at the terminal, in no case a distance of more

than 600 feet. The passenger arriving at a VTOL port and transferring to a

long distance flight, or vice versa, gets into a minibus which shuttles back

and forth between the two ports as demand requires. If passenger demand

justifies it, passenger pods will be available at the VTOL port to eliminate

the shuttle transfer.

Even with the pod system, it will be necessary to provide some

passenger convenience facilities in the terminal for passengers whose cross-

connections are separated by two or three hours. One cannot reasonably

assume that all travelers will be able to schedule connections which will

eliminate waits between flights, and one cannot expect a traveler to sit

quietly in a pod for several hours. It is also very unlikely that any pod will

remain at an airport for such a long period of time. These people will require

lounge areas, restaurant and cocktail facilities, and passenger convenience

facilities and stores. All such facilities are provided on the second floor of

the terminal building, the concourse area. Even with the large passenger flows

expected by 1990, most of the passengers will simply be passing from ground

vehicles to the pods, so that a single terminal building will suffice for lounge

space. Parties greeting arriving travelers or sending-off friends will be dis-

couraged by door fees.

The ground floor of the terminal building serves as the pod platform

area (Figure 5.21). Here rows of pods sit on each side of platforms, the passeng

# GROUND FLOOR

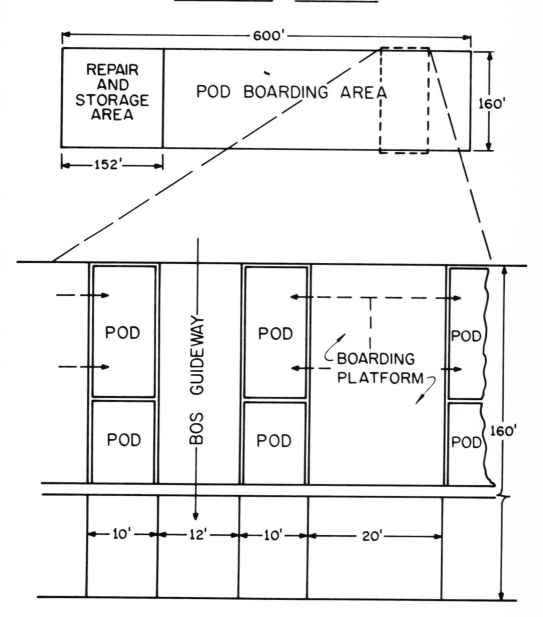

Figure 5.21  Terminal Ground Floor

platforms alternating with lanes for the BOS vehicles. Overhead cranes, each

serving two rows of pods, load the pods onto and off the BOS vehicles, and

the vehicles are carried from the terminal to the runway complex at Brewster

on exclusive guideways shared with cargo-carrying BOS vehicles. The rows

of pods resemble trains at platforms in train stations. The platform is 160 feet

long, permitting 8 pods in a row. Because a plane will hold only 16 pods, a

single platform serves each 500-passenger plane. A passenger flow of 5,000

people per hour during peak hours would require 167 pods per hour if each one

were full. Since many will not be completely full, some additional platform

space must be allowed for extra pods. Allowing almost 50% more spaces than

the hourly peak full-capacity figures would indicate, about 240 pods per hour,

it would take 15 platforms to handle the pods if each pod is in the terminal

for half an hour. Present airplane cleaning times indicate that 30 minutes is

ample time for passenger deboarding, cleaning the pod, and passenger boarding

Sixteen overhead cranes will move the pods, two cranes for each platform pair.

At 240 pods per hour, each crane is assumed to load a pod on or off a BOS

vehicle in four minutes.

The actual pod is shown in Figure 5.22. It is essentially a container

whose dimensions are 20 feet by 9 feet by 8 feet. The end walls bow out to

conform to the sides of the plane. The pod may be loaded on or off BOS

vehicles interchangeably with cargo containers of similar dimensions. (The

cargo pods will not have bowed ends.) The interior of the pod resembles

that of a Boeing 747, or any of the other 500-passenger planes. Seats are

arranged three, four, and three abreast along the length of the pod, with three

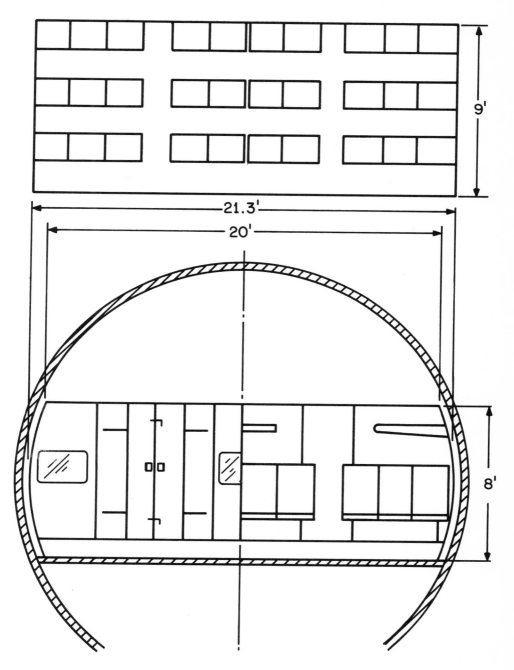

Figure 5.22  Passenger Pod

rows in each pod. When the pod is being carried to the plane by the BOS

vehicle, the seats face sideways to the direction of motion; once the pod

is loaded onto the plane the seats face forward.

The pod has windows on all four walls. The side windows correspond

to windows in the side of the plane once the pod is loaded. The full-length

windows at the end of each aisle at the front and rear of the pod alleviate

claustrophobia during pod maneuvers and the BOS trip. Once the pod is in

position, the windows unlock to become sliding panels permitting passenger

access to other parts of the plane.

The pod is not airtight, relying on pressurization of the plane. However

it should have its own heating and ventilation unit driven from an external

power source. Whenever the pod is occupied, whether in the terminal, on

the BOS vehicle, or in the plane, this unit will be plugged into a power supply

to provide pod air-conditioning. There are no restrooms or galley facilities

in the passenger pods, these functions being provided by a separate module in

the plane.

The interior of the passenger pod is 6 1/2 feet high in the aisles, but

the pod is 8 feet high overall. The extra space is taken up, under the floor,

by baggage drawers. These drawers are actually large bins, with each passen-

ger allotted a baggage space of approximate dimensions 36" by 24" by 18".

Each passenger is restricted to luggage that will fit in such a space, just as

now there are limitations on baggage size.

The pods could be made with thin, strong, honeycomb walls. The interi

would be much like that of current airplanes, with reclining seats at a 34" pitc and 18" off the floor, overhead coat rack and safety equipment compartments,

seats 22" wide and aisles 18" wide. The roof of the pod would have attach-

ment devices for the overhead cranes, and similar lock-down attachments would

be provided in the floor of the pod for securing it to the BOS vehicles and to

the floor of the planes.

In large part, this proposal depends on the development of METRAN

or a similar system in metropolitan areas. The pod system may still be applied

to passenger handling, but more conventional terminal design would be necessary

if the dual-mode BOS vehicle operates only at the airport. The cost estimates

below assume that the airport does not have to develop and maintain a completely

private dual-mode guideway system. Many of the cost estimates for the guide-

way and the vehicles come directly from the METRAN report.

The airport would have to build and maintain only the guideway link

from Logan to Brewster. All other guideway connections to the airport would

be part of the Boston network. At an estimated $2 million per mile, independent

of land costs, the Logan-Brewster guideway would cost $14 million. Land cost

is assumed to be very low, since most of the route is along a public guideway

circling the Harbor.

The terminal building itself is a three-story structure, primarily of

cast-in-place concrete. The top floor, the grid area for the passenger drop-off,

is assumed to be nothing more than a guideway grid with a roof over it. It is

left open to the weather along the sides, since, although it may cause some

passenger discomfort, this plan will not require heating or ventilating a building

through which pass a steady stream of vehicles with internal combustion engines.

The grid is approximately 250 feet by 160 feet, with 4,000 feet of guideway

and 32,000 sq. ft. of platform area. The guideway cost is $400 per linear

foot, and the platform area costs about $14 per sq. ft. Total cost of the upper

floor is therefore approximately $2 million.

The concourse area is 600 feet by 160 feet, or 96,000 sq. ft. At an

estimated $20 per sq. ft. to cover all heating and cooling units, interior

finishing, lighting, etc., the total cost for this floor is approximately $1.9

million. The lower floor is the pod platform area. The guideways for the BOS

vehicles have a total length of about 1500 feet (to include feeder lanes just

outside the building), for a guideway cost of $600,000. The platform areas

occupy 54,000 sq. ft. at approximately $14 per sq. ft. and the extra space

on the lower deck, 24,320 sq. ft. for a total of $1.2 million. The total cost

of the lower floor is $1.8 million. The terminal requires 21 escalator-stairway

combinations at $15,000 each and 16 overhead cranes at $20,000 each. The

total cost of the terminal building is approximately $6.4 million.

The parking garage holds 10,000 cars at an average of 160 sq. ft. per

car. At $20 per sq. ft. to cover all construction and automation costs, this

building costs $32 million.

The airport will need to maintain a fleet of approximately 200 BOS

vehicles to carry the pods and to allow for routine maintenance and repair

of the vehicles. The cost of each vehicle is estimated at $20,000, for a total

cost of $4 million.

The pods will be paid for by the airlines, and so do not involve any

cost to the airport. Their cost is estimated at $10,000 each. Table 5.2 presents

a summary of System II costs. An additional 20% to cover engineering and
contingencies brings the total estimated cost to $67 million.  It should be
remembered that this is the cost of new facilities at Logan only, and does
not include the cost of the runway complex at Brewster.

| ITEM | COST | TOTAL |
|---|---|---|
| Guideway: | | |
| 7 miles of guideway @ $2 million/mi. | $14 million | $14.0 million |
| Station: | | |
| 5,500 feet of guideway @ $400/ft. | $2.2 million | |
| 111,000 sq. ft. platform @ $14/sq.ft. | 1.6 million | |
| 96,000 sq. ft. concourse @ $20/sq.ft. | 1.92 million | |
| 21 escalators @ $15,000 each | 0.32 million | |
| 16 overhead cranes @ $20,000 each | 0.32 million | $ 6.4 million |
| Parking Garage: | | |
| 1,600,000 sq. ft.@ $20/sq.ft. | $32.0 million | $32.0 million |
| BOS Vehicles: | | |
| 200 vehicles @ $20,000 each | $4.0 million | $ 4.0 million |
| | TOTAL | $56.4 million |

Table 5.2  Cost Summary for System II

### 5.6.4  Passenger and Baggage Handling for the V/STOL Ports

If passengers and baggage are processed separately, automated
baggage handling may take a variety of forms, each offering unique advantages.
One possibility is a non-tagged input in which, at a baggage drop point on the
parking level, baggage is merely placed on one of four differently colored
bands of a conveyor, each flight having its own color (for a VTOL unit of up

to 8 pads.) Sorting may be done by machine with baggage destination defined by position on the belt.

In another automated "Red Cap" system, which might be used, one would merely affix a pressure sensitive multi-colored sticker dispensed from a nearby machine to the bag and place it at random on a feeder belt which would carry the bag to the main conveyor. This conveyor would then carry the bags to a sorting station and from there dispatch them to the appropriate plane. Ultimately sorting would be accomplished by means of a color-sensitive optical scanner and other equipment similar to that required for the color-belt system. During early operation, however, sorting might be handled manually and the system converted later in several stages to full automation.

Yet another alternative is the lump system described in Section 5.6.1. In this case colored labels affixed to the lumps would be scanned to send baggage to correct flights.

For any of these systems the baggage sorting on the Handling Floor would proceed similarly. Baggage arriving from the lower level parking floor would be lifted through the mezzanine floor on elevators and queued onto the main conveyor belt linking all modules together. As each bag passes through the appropriate module on the main conveyor, it is selected by a scanner and delivered to the final loading conveyor where loading into the baggage containers takes place. These containers are in turn put into larger standardized containers and transferred by the lifting lounges to the plane where they are loaded directly into the aircraft as the passenger leaves the lounge through a telescoping walkway to take his seat.

Operating speed of a fully automatic conveyor system capable of 60 units per minute gives an average total travel time of about one minute from parking lot to lifting lounge. Bin return ducts operate on call from stations on the lower parking levels to complete the handling cycle.

## 5.7    Access to and between Airport Facilities

To complete our airport design, we turn to the vital question of airport access. In considering access to the Logan Terminal and to our projected Brewster jetport, we deal first with the essential Logan to Brewster link. To provide access to Logan, we recommend a rapid transit system with stops at Logan and the other VTOL terminals, a system designed, however, to serve general city transportation needs. Finally we briefly discuss railway access to the seaport and highway access to the whole harbor area.

### 5.7.1   The Brewster Islands-Logan Terminal Link

For the Brewster jetport to operate with its terminal facilities at Logan the two must be connected by an excellent transportation link. Since this link must be constructed as a first step in this development if it is to serve as an access route for the construction at Brewster, the link must be of a reasonably conventional type, but should be expandable or adaptable to meet future needs.

The estimated peak hour flow on the link for the year 1990 will be about 300 vehicles (of the size of conventional truck trailers) per hour in each direction. This figure is viewed as being high since the peaking factor, the ratio of peak operations to average operations, was assumed to be four, the present figure. It is questionable whether the peaking factor in 1990 will

be this high.

    In view of the reasonably low demand foreseen at least for the near

future, a two lane highway was designed. This highway has extra wide, 15

foot lanes and could be easily converted to an automated system should the

economics of the situation so dictate.

    An automated system was rejected for its much higher initial costs

(probably more than twice those of the proposed system), its high development

costs due to the vehicles' complicated manuevering requirements once on

Brewster, and finally because of anticipated resistance from the Teamsters

Union. A subway-rapid transit type of system was considered and rejected

since it would require a costly and complicated switching network to allow

access by each "train" to every parking location. A monorail system was

rejected for the same reason.

    The route chosen is shown (Figure 5.23). The letters on this drawing

mark off sections; in Table 5.3 cost figures are listed for each of these

sections of the total link. The largest cost will be for the bridge between

Long Island and Deer Island. It should be noted that a tunnel which would

cost about $12 million was also considered but was rejected. Also to be

noted is the bridge connection between Logan and Winthrop; this is planned

to allow access, by pleasure boats, to the seven yacht clubs located between

Logan and Winthrop-East Boston.

    The vehicles using this system will have pneumatic tires, and will,

at least initially, employ drivers. These vehicles will fall into three main

| SECTION | LENGTH (yards) | TYPE OF CONSTRUCTION | COST OF SECTION (in millions) |
|---------|--------|---------------------|----------------|
| AB | 1700 | Road on Land | $1.0 |
| BC | 1200 | Bridge-Causeway | 2.1 |
| CD | 2900 | Road on Land | 1.7 |
| DE | 1600 | High Bridge | 4.5 |
| EF | 2400 | Fill-Causeway | 3.0 |
| FG | 1000 | Road on Land | 0.7 |
| GH | 1000 | Fill-Causeway | 1.5 |
| | | | $14.5 |
| | | 20% for Engineering and Contingencies | 2.9 |
| | | Total Cost | $17.4 |

Cost for a two lane highway, each lane 15 feet wide

Table 5.3 Cost of Bridge from Logan to Brewster

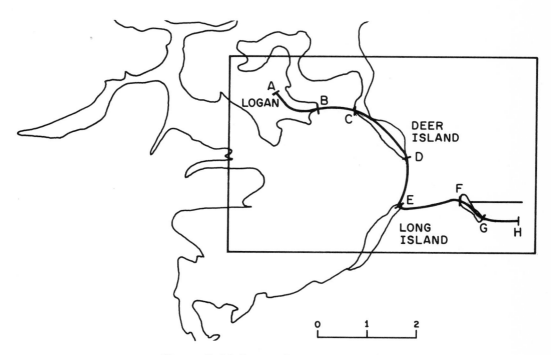

Figure 5.23 Logan-Brewster Link

categories: passenger "buslike" vehicles which will take the passengers from Logan to Brewster, baggage trailers and tractors, and cargo tractors and trailers.

### 5.7.2  Access to Logan

In order to study the economic feasibility of constructing transportation links from the outlying metropolitan area to Logan, a simple model was made. This model included the "access cost" (cost of the time spent by people in coming to the airport), and the cost of constructing the various systems.

Based upon the model used to obtain predictions of total passengers versus year, the total number of passengers per month flying in the years between 1970 and 1990 was computed with access time as a parameter. The results are presented in Figure 5.24. From the numbers of passengers flying,

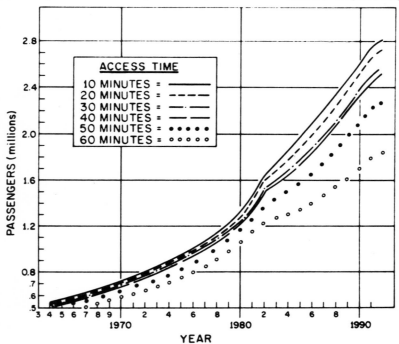

Figure 5.24 Passengers Parametized by Access

and the access time per passenger, assuming an average value of time of

$5/hour, an access cost was determined. To this access cost is added the

approximate cost of building the transportation system which would meet the

access times. These results are summarized in Table 5.4.

A discussion of these figures seems at this point to be in order. In

arriving at these costs the assumption was made that the revenue from each

link would pay for the overhead and debt service, but would not pay for the

initial cost. This assumption was made in view of the extremely low demand

figures for the link. For example, in the year 1980, given a reasonable access

time, there will be about 1.2 million passengers per month flying. Converting

this into long-haul passengers per day, the figure becomes 13,000. Now,

| Home to Brewster Access Time (Minutes) | Long-Haul Passengers 1970-1990 (Millions) | Access Cost Time Valued at $5/Hour (Millions) | Building Cost (Millions) | Total Cost (Millions $) |
|---|---|---|---|---|
| 10 | 11.16 | 92.8 | ? | ? |
| 20 | 10.80 | 180.5 | 500 | 680.5 |
| 30 | 10.32 | 258. | 400 | 658 |
| 40 | 9.81 | 328. | 200 | 528 |
| 50 | 9.38 | 392. | 50 | 442 |
| 60 | 7.92 | 397. | – | 397 |

Schemes used in computing building costs:

| Access Time | Scheme |
|---|---|
| 10 | No system or modified system |
| 20 | Multisation HSGT system |
| 30 | 6 station HSGT link |
| 40 | 2 station HSGT system |
| 50 | Rapid rail |
| 60 | Conventional highway |

Table 5.4 Cost Data for Various Access Schemes

assuming that only one half of these use the link with the remainder coming by car, subway, helicopter, or airplane, the figure shrinks to around 7,000 per day. This figure is just about what a conventional rail-subway system can handle in one half hour. Hence it is very difficult to see how such a system could pay for itself at such low demand figures.

It seems therefore, that a system should not be warrented only as an access system for the airport. If a new system were to be built, it would probably be designed to serve other needs of the general public. With this last statement as a constraint, and with rapid service as a necessity, the system must both have many conveniently located stations, and provide rapid service.

Based on this criterion, the most desirable system would provide break-even operation with rapid service and convenient stations. Such a system would also be much more politically acceptable since the link would not need a subsidy, and would serve the public (this compared to a system which would serve only Logan, and not break even.)

The network for such a recommended system is described in the Glideway Report[7] as a secondary system and is shown here in Figure 5.25. It should be noted that it differs slightly from the system described in the report since there is a terminal serving Logan. This terminal would have to be built under unfavorable geological conditions as described in the report; this problem, however, is not believed to be insurmountable. Terminals will also be located at the VTOL ports. Such a network would cost about $400 million.

---

[7] The Glideway System, M.I.T. Report No. 6, M.I.T. Press, 1965.

It should also be noted that it would be possible to use this type
of system as a freight handling network both for the airport and the seaport
with distribution centers located at one more of the outlying terminals.

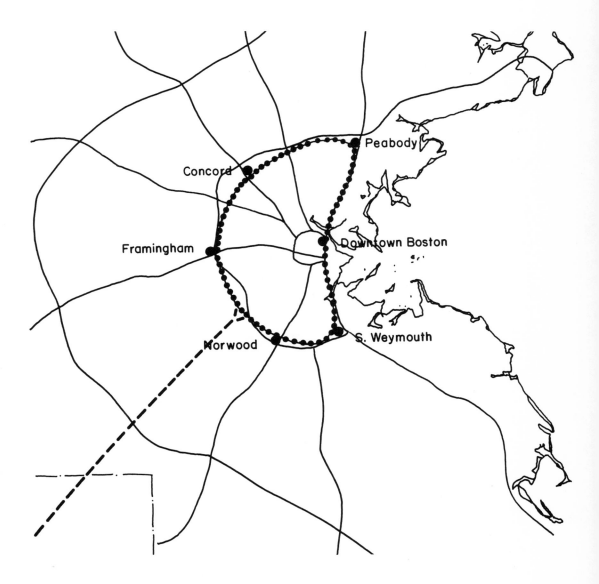

Figure 5.25 Access to Logan

### 5.7.3  Railroad Access to Logan Seaport

In order for the relocated seaport to operate profitably at Logan, a fair amount of cargo must be drawn from and distributed to the Midwest. And since, in the foreseeable future at least, railroad transportation is economically advantageous for long hauls, there must be railway access to the seaport at Logan.

The route of the proposed access is shown in Figure 5.26. The link will be from the railroad yard of the Penn Central over existing track around the corner of the present airport to the seaport area. Also included in this plan is the proposed removal of approximately 2 miles of existing track. The cost of this plan will be about $15 million with the exact cost dependent on the number and length of sidings installed.

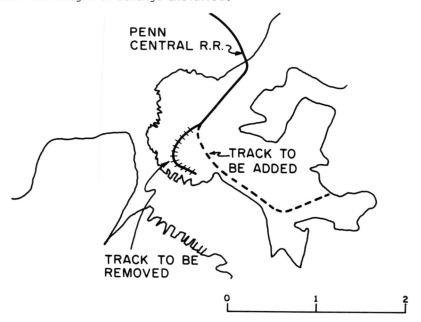

Figure 5.26 Logan Seaport Railroad Access

5.7.4  Harborview Drive

To improve seaport access, a Harborview Drive has been designed and costed. The route would be from Route 3A in Quincy, along the present highway route to the tip of Long Island, across the harbor on a high bridge, allowing ships to pass through, along Deer Island, along Logan Airport to Route C1 in East Boston (Figure 5.27). Again provision has been made for pleasure boats to have uninterrupted access to the sea. It should be noted that while this route runs parallel to the access road to Brewster, the two facilities are separate. The cost of this highway (four lanes) would be $52.5 million (Table 5.5).

| SECTION | LENGTH (yards) | TYPE OF CONSTRUCTION | COST OF SECTION (in millions) |
|---------|----------------|----------------------|-------------------------------|
| AB | 100 | Interchange | $1.0 |
| BC | 4300 | Fill–Causeway | 12.5 |
| CD | 1200 | Bridge–Causeway | 4.2 |
| DE | 2900 | Road on Land | 3.4 |
| EF | 1600 | High Bridge | 9.0 |
| FG | 3100 | Road on Land | 3.6 |
| GH | 850 | Bridge–Causeway | 3.0 |
| HI | 6000 | Road on Land | 7.0 |
| IJ | 100 | Interchange | 1.0 |
|   |   |   | $43.8 |
|   |   | 20% for Engineering and Contingencies | 8.7 |
|   |   | Total Cost | $52.5 |

Table 5.5  Cost of Harborview Drive

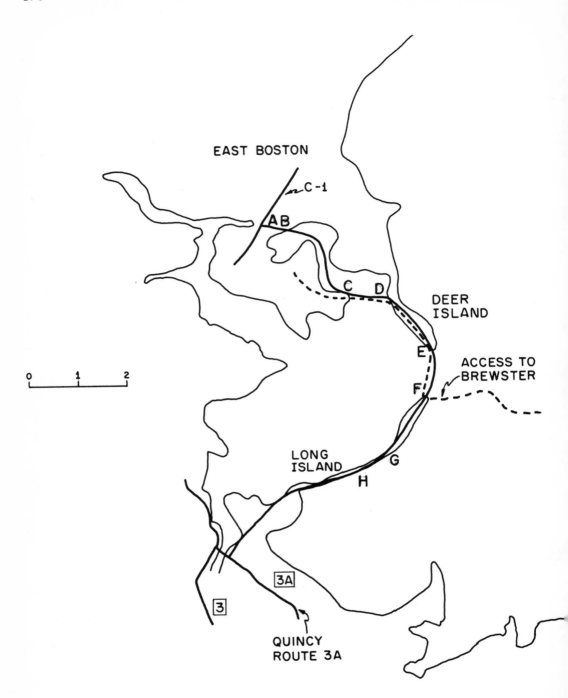

Figure 5.27 Harborview Drive

Chapter 6

THE SEAPORT

This chapter deals in detail with the seaport of Boston: the market
potential of Boston as a port, the products shipped through the port, the
facilities and handling procedures themselves and labor-management
affairs. All of these aspects were considered of major import in the economic
and social analysis leading to our evaluation of Boston as a seaport. Succeeding sections present engineering and construction procedures and costs,
and ultimately, the recommendations for the future of the port. At each
phase of the study, the social and economic investment in the port was
weighed against the potential return to the Boston metropolitan region. This
chapter also presents a broad qualitative indication of the future of the
seaborne transportation industry as well as a quantitative analysis of the
future of Boston as a major port.

Study of the future of the Port of Boston clearly advises that both
the present neglectful course of action and implications of negligent past
decisions and policies seriously endanger the very existence of a seaport
in Boston. The port management's piecemeal, haphazard approach to oper-

ations has encouraged inefficient work practices by the longshoremen,

induced pessimism in the shippers and operators, and endangered long-

term profits. Direct revenue lost to the port operators and indirect loss

from inefficient use of land that should benefit the general public are

the consequences of present operation. Inefficiency is descriptive of the

present Port of Boston in its total spectrum of operations, from the work

procedures of the longshoremen, to the conservative history of the policy

makers. Boston is presently losing its port by default.

As opposed to a continuation of the present policy of operation,

two general alternatives appear advantageous. Although physically they

appear dramatically different, both are concentrated efforts to intensively

utilize the potential of Boston's inner harbor. The first is a deliberate,

gradual elimination of those facilities which are not functioning efficiently,

not returning profits, or are unfit for modern port operations because of

size or location. The remainder of the terminals can then be upgraded and

retained. These, however, represent only a bare skeleton of the present

port and are mainly concentrated in the area of bulk facilities and independ-

ently operated specialty facilities. In either case these terminals are

small and employ only a minimal number of longshoremen. Yet with such

new constraints placed on seaport operations in Boston, specific redevel-

opment plans for the reuse of vacent land can be drawn.

The second general alternative is the construction of a modern,

efficient seaport in the hope of rejuvenating port operations. Such a venture

would require a meaningful change in the administrative structure of the port.

The construction of modern facilities in Boston also represents a substantial investment of both money and effort. The development plan is weighed on one hand against the probability of its success and, on the other, against its potential implications for the Boston metropolitan region. Because of the delicate balance of factors which influence the seaborne transportation industry, our redevelopment plan is highly flexible to allow continual policy evaluation in the light of the constantly changing climate in the industry and the fluctuating position of the Port of Boston relative to the other ports along the East Coast.

Both port alternatives represent cohesive development plans which offer Boston innovative and productive use of its inner harbor resource. These designs reflect comprehensive planning for the long range future of the Port of Boston.

## 6.1    The Value of a Seaport

Transportation systems have evolved greatly from the colonial period when our population was supplied primarily by means of ocean going transport. In the early history of this country, Boston was among the most excellent and prosperous ports. With the passage of time, the faster modes of transportation, rail, truck, airplane, and pipeline have increasingly encroached upon the traditional domination of seaborne shipping. However, oceangoing vessels still serve as an important means of transport, and thus as a part of the urban form. Recent technological developments with respect to ships and to cargo transfer procedures have further enhanced the position of operators and port management alike.

The ship is still the cheapest carrier of low-value bulk cargo. In addition, the advent of containerization has virtually eliminated theft, sped up transfer operations, and revolutionized the concepts of seaborne transportation. Containerization and the increase in ship size and speed have together reduced the costs of transporting general cargo by as much as one tenth and thus enhanced the attractiveness of marine transport of general cargo. Specialty operations from producer to consumer, utilizing the entire ship for cargo destined for one location, have also become a chief contributor to the increase in general cargo tonnage carried by ship.

The modern port benefits the urban community in many respects. Cargo transfer at a port attracts regional trucking, storage and distribution centers. Such activity allows the port community to be a more complete transportation and transfer center and thus represents a substantial economic asset. A seaport originates a great many jobs. A functioning port, even an automated port, will employ more workers than no port at all. In addition to the immediate employment opportunities directly tied to the port, there are secondary opportunities for work in the areas of trucking, storage, and distribution of goods entering the region through the port. The presence of a port will attract port associated industries which will benefit from the existence of its facilities, labor skills, and other environmental conditions: a historical example, during the peak of shipping activities in the Port of Boston, ship building and repairing industries settled in Boston. More important, loss of the seaport will deplete the available labor pool for industries associated with the emerging field of ocean technology.

The port adds a measure of economy, convenience, and safety to the industrial and commercial segment of the population. It allows them the choice of transportation facilities from the total range available. The supplies and raw materials for the metropolitan region are not restricted to overland travel. A port fosters an increased flow of goods through the region. In fact one measure of the prosperity of a community is the volume of goods passing through its transportation terminals. It has been estimated that each ton of general cargo adds $6 to the economy of the region. Last, a port has distinct esthetic appeal. A modern, operating seaport delights the eye, educates the mind, and quickens a feeling for historic sea lore.

Thus a port can contribute to the over-all prosperity and physical form of its city, but of course these benefits are not without cost. A port must be physically connected both to the local storage and distribution centers and to the outbound expressway and railway systems leading to other parts of the country. It must be equipped and manned so as to successfully compete with other ports and other means of transportation. Often the facility requirements demand the investment of substantial amounts of capital and additional commitments of both time and effort. In particular, the operation of a seaport requires extremely delicate decisions to be made, particularly in the field of labor relations. But as has been proven with the successful modernization of the Port of New York with its Elizabeth, New Jersey container facilities, a port can overcome such difficulties.

The wide range of prosperity in this country's ports is not unlike the climate in many of our national industries which vie for a restrictive market. Some flourish while others barely subsist. Although geographical assets vary, with seaports as with industries, this inequality primarily reflects the management of each port, and its ability to make correct decisions at the appropriate time. As in other aspects of the American economy, ports represent an inherently free-enterprise operation, where individual communities attempt to attract shippers and operators to their facilities.

To a city with a port tradition, much more is at stake than the simple transfer of cargo within city boundaries. Once lost, the history and customs of a way of life can never be revived. Boston's port facilities have been placed in serious jeopardy. The question remains whether or not management can make the decisions required to salvage the Port of Boston.

## 6.2    The Present Port of Boston

The Port of Boston is indeed a center of activity, but it is essentially wasted activity. Gangs of over a hundred men spend days unloading a ship that ten men could handle in a few hours. Such practices maintain the high cost of shipping through Boston. Dollies and forklifts have survived the advent of container cranes (Figure 6.1). Old and rotting piers occupy land far too valuable for such waste.

A hoard of outmoded procedures and facilities are taking their toll on the profits of the port administration and the total tonnage (general) moving through the port. In 1956 1,221 vessels carrying general cargo entered the Port of Boston. This number rose to 1,417 in 1960 but by 1967 had dropped to 1,114. The total tonnage of foreign and domestic imports

Figure 6.1
Antiquated Cargo Handling Methods

and exports remained almost constant during the period 1961-1966 at a level of 20,000,000 short tons.[1] In the extreme case, shippers have discontinued use of the Boston port, and have eliminated Boston from their schedule. The departure of United States Lines in 1968 was met with quiet expectation by both longshoremen and port management.

No active effort is presently being made to rectify the situation. Complacent union labor uses new handling procedures only in return for short term gains of a guaranteed annual wages, a situation which in the long run endangers the port's existence and the security of workers' jobs. Likewise the port management and other decision-makers allow rising port costs to the shipper to take their toll.

The harbor falls far short of being a center of pride for the community. In many respects it is a visual disgrace. Refuse and waste disposal into the water creates a serious pollution problem. The present situation appears more reprehensible when one considers that we have neither an effective

---

[1] 1968/1969 Transportation Facts for the Boston Region, the Boston Redevelopment Authority, September 1, 1968.

seaport nor beneficial use of the waterfront land in the inner harbor.

The port presently occupies facilities throughout the inner harbor
(Figure 6.2). Bulk facilities, particularly for petroleum and storage, are

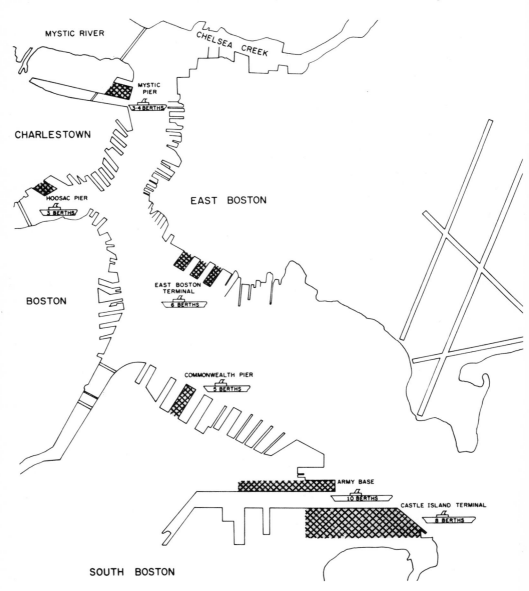

Figure 6.2 Present Port Facilities

concentrated in the lower Chelsea Creek area of the Inner Harbor. The

general cargo terminals are scattered throughout the remaining areas.

The Inner Harbor passage is constricted by narrow, convoluted channels

with little or no room for turn-abouts and other necessary ship manoeuvers.

The facilities themselves are unfit for modern cargo transfer operation,

because of location, lack of adequate marshalling facilities, and the

narrow and restrictive aprons and piers. The traditional finger piers,

gradually replaced by the more efficient and safer marginal piers in other

ports, are still in evidence throughout the harbor.

The sole exception to the above description of facilities in Boston

Harbor is Castle Island. It is equipped with a $3 million container crane

(Figure 6.3), along with more than adequate marshalling and storage area.

Figure 6.3 Castle Island Container Crane

Yet because of labor disputes it had never been used prior to April 1969.

It rests idle today despite labor reform due to the current wishes of

Sea-Land, Inc., which owns the facilities. Even this, most modern facility

in the Harbor, is not adequately connected either to the city's storage

and distribution areas, or to the expressway system. Castle Island, as

the rest of the port facilities, is designed to feed directly to city streets.

This constellation of problems in today's port cries for reconsid-

eration of current policies and programs designed for the port's future.

The following sections present the procedure we used to assess the potential

of the port and to determine further recommendations.

6.3   Economic Analysis Procedure

In order to find a solution to the complex problem of the seaport of

Boston, it is important to isolate the critical issues and important parameters

of a port and to evaluate all feasible alternatives. Although our emphasis

was primarily on economic variables or variables easily translated into eco-

nomic terms, these were far from the only source of criteria. A revision of

port policy must endure against prevailing pressures and also adapt to unan-

ticipated future conditions; to that end a plan of development must foresee

beneficial use of harbor resources for many years to come. The target date

for Project BOSPORUS is 1990.

After parameters and alternatives were explored in depth a decision

procedure was constructed. As an aid to predicting the outcome of various port policies a mathematical model of the port was developed which helped

to evaluate alternatives on a common economic basis. The model was not,

however, a decision maker, rather it was used as a tool to evaluate possible

policy or alternative development strategies.

Throughout the study the major assumption made was that if port

charges in Boston can be lowered sufficiently, then the predicted potential

demand will in fact become real. Underlying this assumption is the principle

that shippers will use the mode of transportation that offers them the cheap-

est over-all cost.

The range of alternatives considered was as all-inclusive as possible

and varied from the immediate closing of the port to a massive redevelopment

plan. The following is a list of the alternatives considered:

1) Close down the port

2) Use M.P.A. land (as at present), upgrading facilities

3) Share Logan land, airport retains present functions

4) Use Castle Island with container facilities

5) Use modernized Army Base

6) Build a seaport at Squantum

7) Build a seaport at Logan; replace CTOL port with VTOL port

8) Build a seaport at Brewster operating jointly with the new Airport

9) Leave the situation unchanged

10) Various combinations of the above

Some of the above were discarded as technically unfeasible. For
example, operating a seaport in conjunction with an airport for conventional
aircraft which would take-off and land in the vicinity was ruled out because
of problems of physical interference between ships and aircraft. Others
were eliminated due to present land use, lack of marshalling space, and
inflexibility for container operations. The remaining alternatives were evaluated on the bases of facility cost, ability to satisfy market needs, profitability, and manpower levels.

The procedure used to determine the optimal alternative from an
economic standpoint was the following:

1) Determine the total market potential

2) Model the port with the market, costs, facilities, and employment levels and port policies as inputs

3) Evaluate alternatives to determine steady state results and
   long term advantages.

4) Establish the transient costs --- money invested while the
   return on investment is not yet positive

5) Evaluate sites and physical facilities needed, as well as
   capacity

6) Generate development alternative

7) Evaluate alternative with respect to other bases of judgment

8) Propose plan with engineering designs and construction costs
   and schedules

9) Compare results to other alternatives

The following sections describe in detail this economic analysis as well as the other bases of judgment.

## 6.4    The Prediction Model

One uses a mathematical model in an evaluation process because,
if the relationships among all of the important variables are properly defined
in the problem, the model can predict the results of a decision over a period
of time in the future. Thus in a short period of time various alternatives can
be evaluated with the aid of this mathematical device. On an absolute basis,
the results cannot be assumed infallible because an important variable may
not have been included. In a relative sense, however, when one compares
a range of alternatives, a mathematical model is extremely effective in
ordering the alternatives from best to worst.

The Port of Boston was analyzed and divided into various sectors
representing all of the important aspects of port operation. A model relating
these sectors was then programmed in DYNAMO computer language[2]. It was run
to compare various alternatives such as port location, labor policies, and facility building rates. Figure 6.4 depicts the function and output of the computer
model. Into the model we fed potential port policies, cost of an alternative,
and the present value of port costs, tonnage, facilities, and number of men
employed. The model then predicted over a range of years from 1968 to 1990 the

---

[2] Alexander L. Pugh III, DYNAMO User's Manual, 2nd Ed., M.I.T. Press,
Cambridge, Mass., 1963.

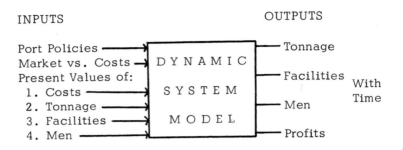

Figure 6.4  Computer Model

expected tonnage, facilities, number of men employed, and profits to the port

administration.  In this way alternatives could be compared.

Figure 6.5 presents a simplified model for the Port of Boston as deter-

mined  by our analysis.  It was ascertained that the port operations divide into

five major sectors: facilities sector, labor sector, market sector, shipper cost

sector, and port financial sector.  The influence of each of these sectors upon

the others is depicted in the same figure.  For example, the number of facilities

influences the number of men employed which in turn determines the port costs,

the shippers' cost, and indirectly the market size for the Port of Boston.

Figure 6.6 presents in greater detail the components and factors contained in

each of the five sectors.  The facilities sector comprises the number and types

of facilities in the port, the projected building rate, and the efficiency of ter-

minals.  The labor sector computes the number and productivity of men employed

by the port management.  The market sector reviews the total tonnage handled

and potential market size, while the shipper cost sector adds the components

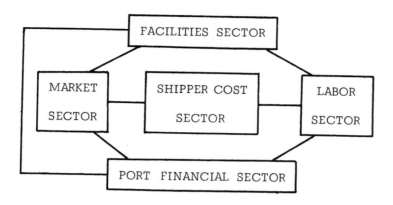

Figure 6.5  Port of Boston Model

of the shippers' cost, cargo waiting costs, in-port cost, handling costs, and

transportation costs to determine the total over-all cost to the shipper.  Last,

the port financial sector weighs each of the preceding sectors and calculates

the port profits from the revenue, operating expenses, cost of labor, and building

costs.  Finally, Figure 6.7 illustrates more clearly the relationships among the

various parts of the model.  Notice how such a model resembles the actual oper-

ation of the port.  For example, if the handling costs are lessened, following

the arrow, the total in-port costs also decrease, thus enabling the potential

market size to grow.  As, after a period of time, the potential market increases,

so does the tonnage through the port and in turn the number of workers at the

piers and so on.

In its final form, the model predicted the important results and divided

the costs for various interested parties: the shippers, the operators, the admin-

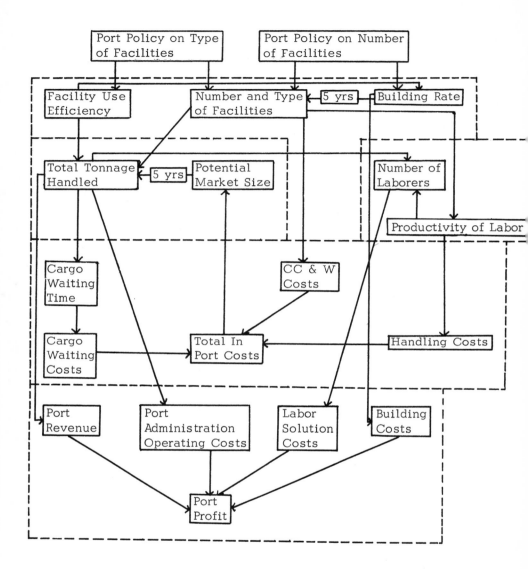

Figure 6.6 Detailed Port Model

istration, and the workers. For each of the alternatives the number of berths, or size of facilities, could be predicted for each of the next 22 years.  The

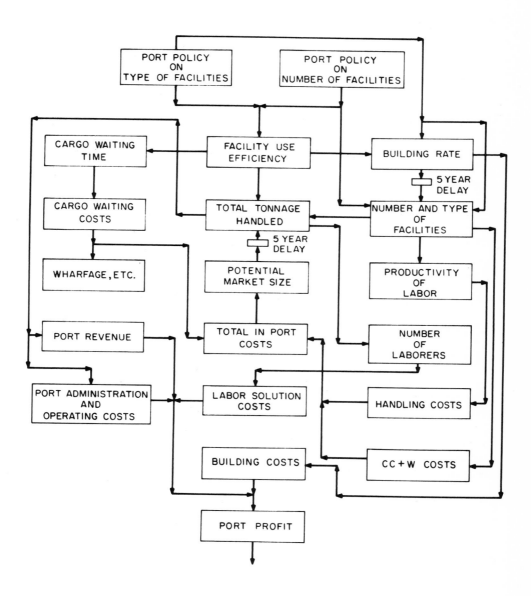

Figure 6.7  Detailed Port Model

costs to the administration, and the numbers of jobs available were also
indicated. Thus, despite its inherent limitations, the model proved extremely useful. The next portion of the analysis sought to determine the market
potential of the Port of Boston.

## 6.5    The Boston Market Potential

The market of the Port of Boston is the number of tons of material
shipped through the port. The potential market is the number of tons that
could be shipped through the port if conditions in Boston were favorably
altered. In the most optimistic (and unrealistic) case, all of the products
shipped to and from the United States East Coast could be shipped through
Boston under a proper set of conditions, for example, if Boston were the
only port. To determine the realistic potential market, one must augment
the real market presently shipping through Boston by estimates of Boston's
possible share of three other markets: all goods dispatched through competing East Coast ports, all goods shipped from the East Coast by competing modes, and last, new tonnage generated by growth of the industrial
base in Boston's vicinity.

Discounting minor factors which influence shippers' routing
decisions, such as availability of banking facilities and predetermined
loyalties, for all of the above cases the potential market size may be
increased primarily by lowering the total cost of shipping through Boston.
The total shipping cost includes: the cost of transportation to and from the
port, port expenses and charges, the cost of the trip by ship, and the time
of the trip including the time spent waiting in the port. The cost for waiting

time is computed as a depreciation of the goods on a daily basis. For

example, if the products take ten days longer to be shipped from Boston

than from a competing port, the waiting cost is 3%[3] per year times 10 days

times the value of the cargo.

If the costs of various ports, including waiting cost, are plotted

against tonnage through the port, a remarkably predictable curve results.

It is pictured in Figure 6.8. Note that one extreme is the total volume of

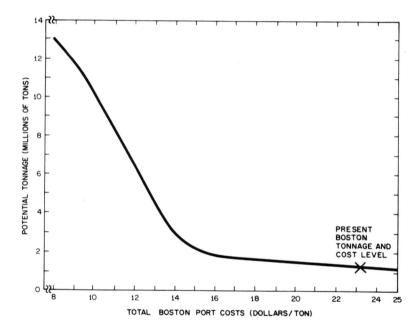

Figure 6.8 Port Costs Vs. Tonnage

trade now carried by ship from the East Coast ports; at the other extreme

the curve asymptotically approaches zero. Observe the position of Boston.

_____

[3] A very conservative estimate of port waiting cost; even with a figure this
low, the total port costs are still unconscionably high.

This low position presents planners with an enormous potential market that is presently making other competing ports profitable, while Boston is only shipping the minimum number of tons. It should be noted that the situation in Boston is so extremely disadvantageous that many New England shippers prefer to send their products by truck to New York and bypass the Port of Boston. In addition, the model assumes today's conditions; in the future we can expect continued growth in the productivity of this country's industries and consequently an increase in the number of tons of material shipped by sea routes.

To determine how much port charges in Boston must be reduced to receive a greater portion of the market, one must first consider the geographical position of the Port of Boston. Boston enjoys the distinct advantage of proximity to the Atlantic shipping lanes. In addition, it is 200 miles closer to Europe than any of the other major East Coast ports. This differential amounts to a 30¢ per ton advantage for the Port of Boston. However, this cost reduction is balanced by the increased cost of land transportation to all shippers located outside of New England. Further, the waiting time cost in the Port of Boston is large compared to other ports. This is, however, primarily due to the small market of the present Boston port. If the market grows, then operators can be convinced to ship to Boston more often with the direct result of lowering the waiting cost and hence the total cost even further.

We can calculate which traffic Boston may expect to receive after reducing total through port costs by examining to which operators it can offer a lower price. For example, if the trucking cost between Boston and

Pittsburg is $7.60 per ton higher than between Philadelphia and Pittsburgh,

and Boston's total in port costs including waiting costs are $6.80 more

than those of Philadelphia, then Boston would have to lower its through

port costs by $14.40 per ton to draw traffic from Pittsburgh. The shipper

could also be offered an attractive portion of the 30¢ per ton ship travel

savings.

    Boston was compared to ports which compete for the trade generated

in the eastern part of the country with various rate differentials. These

differentials represent the difference in cost between Boston and the lowest

cost port of the particular area in question (Table 6.1). In other words,

| SHIPPER'S CITY | TRUCKING COST DIFFERENTIAL ($/TON)* |
|---|---|
| SYRACUSE | $1.60 |
| BUFFALO | 1.80 |
| PITTSBURGH | 7.60 |
| CLEVELAND | 5.00 |
| COLUMBUS | 7.60 |
| CINCINNATI | 7.60 |
| DETROIT | 5.00 |
| INDIANAPOLIS | 6.00 |
| LOUISVILLE | 7.20 |
| CHICAGO | 3.80 |
| MILWAUKEE | 3.80 |
| ST. LOUIS | 5.00 |

* Supplementary cost of trucking to Boston rather
   than to nearest port

Table 6.1 Shippers' Cost Differential

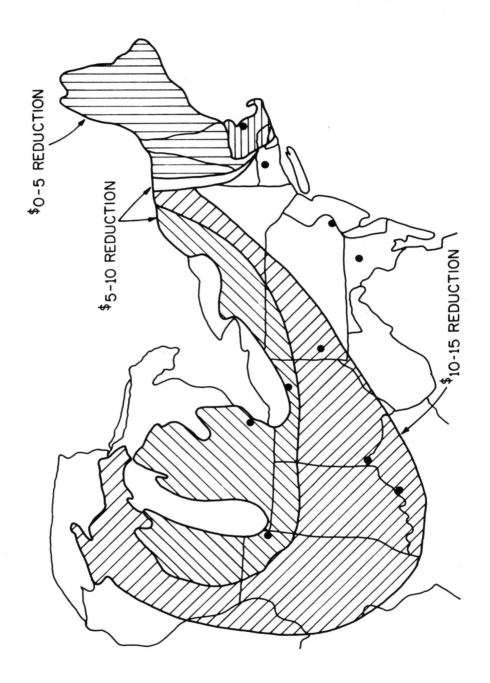

Figure 6.9  Port of Boston Potential Market

if Boston could lower its cots by $14.40 it would then attract the trade of

Pittsburgh away from Philadelphia. A map was made of the cost differentials

and the reflected increase in potential market size. Boston would attract

the striped area in Figure 6.9 with a zero to $5 reduction. The dotted area

represents a $10 to $15 reduction in the total rates charged in Boston. The

The cross-hatched area is the immediate hinterland of the Boston port where

it enjoys a present favorable cost differential.

To the growth of market potential due to attracting trade from the

other ports, one must add additional trade drawn from other modes of trans-

portation and new trade generated by regional development. These supple-

ments were found nearly impossible to predict; however, they would certainly

make the port situation in Boston even more favorable than that projected

by our study of a single source of potential market. In addition, the following

plan for the development of the Port of Boston offers ample flexibility to adjust

the number of berths available to accommodate such unforeseen increases in

market size.

The information on the potential market for the Port of Boston was

used as an input to the model to determine market size, and in turn, what

facilities are required by various policy alternatives. The following section

describes the physical alternatives possible; it is succeeded by an evaluation

of alternatives.

## 6.6    Seaport Site Alternatives

This section considers the physical alternatives possible, rather than

designs or development plans for any one location. It surveys the Boston harbor area and evaluates potential sites for a new seaport in the region.

The wide range of alternatives open to policy makers is constrained chiefly by geographical factors. The prime requisite of a port is a waterfront location. Boston fortunately possesses large tracts of unused acreage along the ocean, close to the commercial centers of the city and to the expressway system.

The physical requirements for super-ships, which must be attracted to ensure the economic development of a port, differ vastly from the traditional piers and channels utilized by the smaller ships which frequent the Port of Boston today. The super-ships demand a wide channel near to shipping lanes with adequate areas for turning. The shortest trip to the pier is the most desirable. The pier itself should be a marginal pier featuring large aprons with land based container cranes. Such an arrangement contrasts sharply with the finger piers and shipboard cranes in operation today.

The new method of cargo handling, although cheaper and more efficient, needs from 15 to 25 acres per berth for marshalling and storage facilities. The docking area itself must be protected from winds, waves and high tides. The harbor's fine sheltered areas presently used for port operations are in some cases inimical to modern port operation because of their location deep in the heart of the harbor. The optimal location is sheltered but easily accessible to shipping lanes. Similarly, port facilities must link directly to inland areas by safe and efficient highways, preferably reserved for only the truck traffic generated by the port.

A number of promising areas lie in the vicinity of Boston harbor. The

Port Authority presently owns two such sites: Castle Island and the Army Base. Logan Airport presently occupies a third location, but the construction of a new airport in the outer harbor would free the Logan site for alternative development. A fourth area whose distance from primary shipping lanes diminishes its desirability, is a large stretch of land between Quincy and Squantum, to be called the Squantum site in the remainder of the report. This land formerly housed the Naval Reserve Aviation Base and is presently occupied by the Boston Marina and by storage facilities of the Jordan Marsh Company. Boston is indeed fortunate in having four potential development sites for a modernized container seaport within eight miles of the central business district and less than three miles from the main interstate routes of the region.

Other areas were also considered, but eliminated because of either technical or other constraints. The inner harbor area to the West and North of the mouth of Presidents' Roads was rejected because of inaccessability to shipping lanes and inadequate space for a proper turn-around of the vessels. We discarded points in the outer harbor as too near to and therefore incompatible with a new airport in the outer harbor. A modern cargo ship boasts a top mast of up to 168 feet above sea level which would interfere with the landing and take-off of aircraft at the airport. Other locations in the general harbor district were discounted because of the excess cost of dredging additional channels.

Both the ship owners and the construction planners should find the remaining sites acceptable. With judicious highway planning each of the four port locations can, with relative ease, be connected to both the North

and South arteries of the city. The locations are differentiated primarily by

the number of ships each can berth. Castle Island and the Army Base are

the smallest, but also represent the lowest capital investment. The Logan

site could be developed into a major seaport, affording harborage to over

20 ships at one time. In addition, this location offers the advantage of a

circular basin in which the ships would move only in one direction, thereby

removing the need for the turn-around procedure. The Squantum site can

accommodate 12 ships at one time, but it is less accessible than Logan and

a substantial amount of dreding would be required to widen Nantasket Roads

for large commercial ships.

Castle Island, the Army Base, Logan Airport, and the Squantum site

were each introduced into the computer model as possible locations for the

development alternatives. The evaluation of the four practicable seaport sites,

as based on this model, is presented in section 6.7.

## 6.7    Evaluation of Alternatives with the Model

The present port situation, the market potential, and the location of

available sites - the information set forth in the previous three sections -

were given as primary inputs to the computer model. This section outlines

the procedure used to ascertain the costs of developing the seven major

alternatives considered and offers the final results of the model evaluation.

The first basis of comparison is the cost for development of each of

the sites versus the requirements as determined by the market potential section of the model. Figure 6.10 presents land costs for variable amounts of acreage,

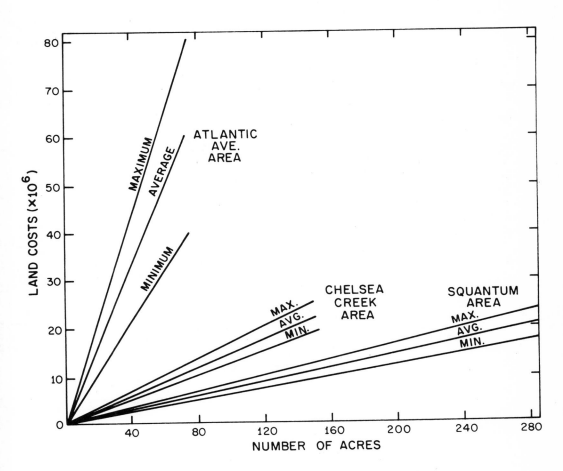

Figure 6.10  Land Costs for Variable Acreage Amounts

either undeveloped or subject to purchase and alteration, in different parts

of the harbor. The next two graphs, Figures 6.11 and 6.12 present the costs

first of a general cargo facility, and second for a container terminal. The

construction costs are broken down into apron and piling costs, and paving

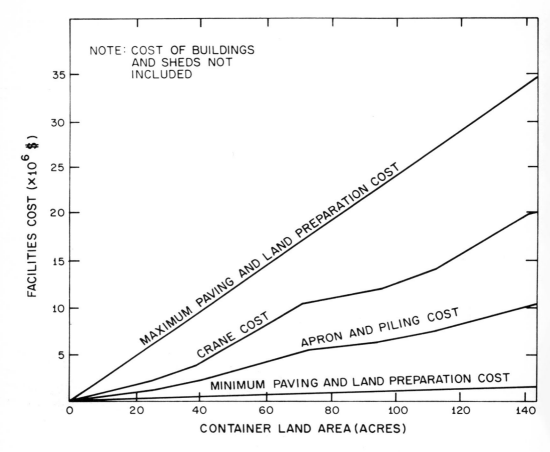

Figure 6.11 Costs of a General Cargo Facility

costs. The considerable variation in paving land preparation costs reflects the large variance in soil conditions and bedrock location. These three graphs were used in determining the cost of a seaport development at all of the locations under consideration.

The seven tables, Table 6.2 through Table 6.8, present in summary form the total costs for development of each of the seven major design alternatives. The first possibility is to close down the general cargo port, leaving only bulk and specialty facilities in operation. Income from sale

of Port Authority land would amount to $70 million which if invested at 4%

per year would return a profit of $2.8 million per year. If the capital were

invested at 10% it would return $7 million per year. Both of these figures

compare favorably to the present port profit of only $1 million per year.

The second major alternative is to close down the port, save for bulk and

specialty facilities and Castle Island. The revenue from the sale of land

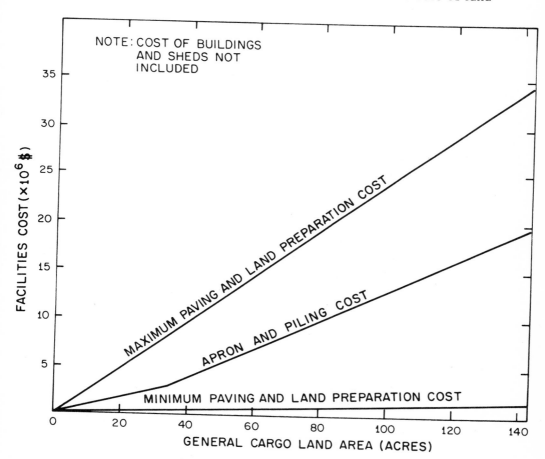

Figure 6.12  Costs of a Container Terminal

Alternative I: Close Down Port (Except for Bulk Facilities)

    Income from Sale of
    Port Land (Except Castle Island)
    ($15/ft$^2$) x 100 Acres                    $60 Million

    Income from Sale of
    Castle Island                              $10 Million

                              Total          $70 Million

    Net Income = $70 Million Invested at 6%/Year = $4.2 Million/Year


                    Table 6.2  Alternative I



Alternative II:  Close Down Port (Except for Castle Island and Bulk)

    Income
        Proceeds from Sale of
        Port Land (Except Castle Island)  $60 Million
        Cost of Additional Facilities     $ 6 Million

                          Net Proceeds    $54 Million

        Income on Net Proceeds of
        $54 Million @ 6% per year          $3.2 Million/Year
        Income from Wharfage (Usage
        and Dockage)Charges
        800,000 tons @ $2.25/ton          $1.8 Million/Year

                          Total Income    $5.4 Million/Year

    Expenses
        Administration and Operating
        Costs                             $0.3 Million/Year
        Cost of Labor Solution            $0.7 Million/Year

                          Total Expenses  $1.0 Million/Year

                Net Income = $4.4 Million/Year


                    Table 6.3  Alternative II

Alternative III:  Maintain Port as at Present

Income
Income from Wharfage, etc.
1 Million Tons @ $2.25/ton        $ 2.25 Million/Year

Expenses
Administration and Operating
Costs                             $ 1.0   Million/Year

Net Income = $1.25 Million/Year

Table 6.4  Alternative III

would amount to $60 million.  Of this, $6 million would be utilized to build

additional facilities.  If the remainder were invested it would yield an annual

interest of $3.2 million.  One must add to this interest the income from

wharfage charges for the 800,000 tons that the facility potentially could

continue to transfer each year.  Subtracted from these totals are the port

operation expenses and the cost of a solution to the labor problem.  This

alternative would return approximately $4.4 million to the managing authority

per year.

The third alternative is to maintain the port as presently operated

with a net revenue of $1.25 million per year.  The fourth alternative is the

use of the Army Base alone.  It would return a profit of approximately $5.2

million, while the fifth alternative, construction of a seaport using 10%

of Logan Airport's land, would return $7.4 million to the management

authority.  A sixth alternative, a new seaport at Squantum, would return

approximately $4 million each year.  The final combined development

Alternative IV: Army Base Alone

    Income
       Proceeds from Sale of Port
       Land (Including Castle Island)    $60 Million
       Cost of New Facilities
       (Detailed in Table 6.9)         $ 6 Million

                    Net Proceeds    $53.75 Million

       Income on Net Proceeds of
       $53.75 Million @ 6% per year    $ 3.2 Million/Year
       Income from Wharfage, etc.
       1.3 Million Tons @ $2.25/ton   $ 2.9 Million/Year

                    Total Income    $ 6.1 Million/Year

    Expenses
       Administrative and Operating
       Costs                   $ 1.1 Million/Year

          Net Income = $5.0 Million/Year

            Table 6.5 Alternative IV

Alternative V: Utilization of 10% of Logan Site (200 Acres) Alone

    Income
       Proceeds from Sale of Port
       Land (Including Castle Island
       and Army Base) - 115 Acres    $70. Million
       Cost of New Facilities
          Paving and Access Roads    $ 6.0 Million
          Bulkhead, Piling, and
          Dredging Costs        $19.0 Million
          30 Container Cranes
          Including Foundations, etc.   $15.0 Million
          Storage Sheds         $ 3.5 Million
          Miscellaneous         $ 1.5 Million
          Engineering, Financial
          Aid and Legal Fund       $ 5.0 Million
               Total Cost    $50. Million

              Net Proceeds    $20. Million

Alternative V: Utilization of 10% of Logan Site Alone (Continued)

Income
    Income on Net Proceeds of
    $20 Million @ 6% per year       $ 1.2 Million/Year
    Income for Wharfage, etc.
    4 Million Tons @ $2.25/ton      $ 9.0 Million/Year

              Total Income    $10.2 Million/Year

Expenses
    Administration and Operating
    Costs                      $ 1.5 Million/Year
    Cost of Labor Solution       $ 0.5 Million/Year

              Total Expenses  $ 2.0 Million/Year

        Net Revenue = $8.2 Million/Year

Table 6.6 Alternative V

Alternative VI: Build New Facility at Squantum,
                Close Down Port (Except Bulk)

Income
    Proceeds from Sale of Port Land  $70.0 Million
    Cost of New Facilities
        Land Cost (250 Acres)     $18.0 Million
        Paving (200 Acres @
        $1/sq.ft.               $ 8.0 Million
        Apron and Piling Costs    $19.6 Million
        Dredging              $ 7.5 Million
        Crane Costs           $10.0 Million
        Access                $ 8.0 Million
        Shed Cost             $ 1.0 Million
        Miscellaneous         $ 4.0 Million
        Engineering, Financial,
        Aid and Legal Fund      $ 7.5 Million
              Total Cost  $88.0 Million

            Ned Proceeds  -$18.0 Million

Income from Wharfage, etc.
3 Million Tons @ $2.25/ton     $ 6.75 Million/Year

             Total Income   $ 6.75 Million/Year

Alternative VI: Build New Facility at Squantum (Continued)

Expenses
Yearly Cost to Pay Back $18
Million deficit in 40 Years
@ 6%; $18 Million x 0.067[*]                   $ 1.2 Million/Year
Administration and Operating
Costs                                          $ 1.5 Million/Year
Cost of Labor Solution                         $ 0.5 Million/Year

                            Total Expenses   $ 3.2 Million/Year

                  Net Revenue = $3.5 Million/Year

                  Table 6.7 Alternative VI


Alternative VII: Castle Island, Army Base and 10% Logan

Income
Proceeds from Sale of Port Land
(Excluding Castle Island, Army Base)           $50. Million
Cost of New Facilities
    See Alternatives II, IV, and V
    For Breakdown                              $62.2 Million
                          Net Proceeds        -$12.2 Million
Income from Wharfage, etc.
6.1 Million Tons @ $2.25/ton                   $13.7 Million/Year

                            Total Income       $13.7 Million/Year

Expenses
Yearly Cost to Pay Back $12.2 Million
$12.2 Million x 0.067[*]                        $ 0.8 Million/Year
Administration and Operating Costs             $ 3.0 Million/Year
Cost of Labor Solution                         $ 0.6 Million/Year
                            Total Expenses     $ 4.4 Million/Year

                  Net Revenue = $9.3 Million/Year

* The indicated Capital Recovery Factor of 0.067 represents a repayment period of 40 years at an interest rate of 6%, or a period of
approximately 29 years at 5%.

                  Table 6.8 Alternative VII

alternative would return the greatest profit of all, over $9 million per year.

For the different alternatives the model also predicted employment

levels, tonnages, facilities, and numbers of berths. They are presented in

summary form in Figure 6.13. It can be seen that from all of the economic

criteria the combined alternative appears the most favorable.

| Alternatives | Tonnage (Millions) | Men | Yearly Profits (Millions) | Facilities Cost (Millions) | Container Berths | General Cargo Berths |
|---|---|---|---|---|---|---|
| Close Port (I) | 0 | 0 | 4.2 | 0 | 0 | 0 |
| Do Nothing (III) | 1 | 1,000 | 1.25 | 0 | 0 | 26-33 |
| Components | | | | | | |
| A. Castle Is. (II) | .8 | 80 | 4.0 | 6 | 4 | 0 |
| B. Army Base (IV) | 1.3 | 40 (cont.) | | | | |
| | | 300 (G.C.) | 5.0 | 6.25 | 3 | 5 |
| C. 10% Logan (V) | 4 | 500 | 8.2 | 50 | 20 | 0 |
| D. Squantum (VI) | 3 | 450 | 3.5 | 88 | 18 | 0 |
| Castle Island, Army Base, and Logan (VII) | 6.1 | 1,300 | 9.3 | 62.2 | 24 | 7 |

Figure 6.13 Summary of Port Alternatives

The forecast model indeed offers significant predictions: they sustain

the belief that port operation in the future in Boston is not only possible, but

also profitable, returning more to the port management than is presently collec-

ted, while at the same time handling more tons of cargo and employing a much

larger labor force. In section 6.8 other indicators and bases of comparison

challenge this optimism. Then the following two sections present the optimum

time schedule and the engineering aspects of the plan.

6.8     Other Bases of Comparison

The model served to establish a comparison among the various
development alternatives dictated by economic considerations. Yet other
sets of criteria must also assist as bases of judgment in planning for the
future of the seaport in Boston. The economic profitability of the seaport
is no greater in importance than the results any design would have on the
physical resource of the Boston Harbor.

Numerous unanswerable questions arose and formed a set of attitudes which influenced the final decisions. Is the long range future of
ocean transportation promising or is seaborne transportation merely a rem-
nant of the past? Should a large scale investment in the present port be
undertaken while the future of the maritime industry as a whole remains
in question? Will seaport Harbor development preempt other necessary
additions to the Boston urban form? Will the increased activity prevent
enjoyment of the harbor resource as a recreation facility? Is the Harbor
going to be used to its potential? With the addition of a seaport, will the
safety and pollution problems of the Harbor increase ? On the other hand,
will the elimination of the port cause Boston to become only a distant
suburb of New York with respect to transportation facilities? Would the
extinction of the Boston seaport permanently disqualify Boston from being
a first rate transportation and, therefore, economic center?

Such questions and many others were examined in the hope of
developing a comprehensive plan, one which would provide all of the
necessary components not only for successful port operation, but also for

other satisfying aspects of urban living. Such questions were used as

limiting cases of the development alternatives and to evaluate the results

of the harbor closing alternative; the intangible values thus developed

within our group gave vision to the constraints of large scale planning and

development.

Boston is again at a crossroads. In one direction it can accept its

diminishing seaport activity and employ the harbor resource as a recreation

and urban development locus; thereby is severed the tradition of Boston's

seaport. Or, Boston can take calculated risks to develop a modern port

within its Harbor while minimizing the danger to other conceivable harbor

developments. The two alternatives are presented in depth in the next two

sections.

## 6.9    The Optimal Development Alternative

The analysis appraising market potential and development costs

proclaimed feasible indeed a modern seaport for Boston. From selected

locations and the model's projected timetable, a detailed development alter-

native was then fashioned. This redevelopment proposal is our prime recom-

mendation for the future seaport and Boston.

Construction of new facilities cannot begin until a solution to the

labor problem is devised. Furthermore, the new port management system

must be adopted. Only after the successful completion of both these reforms

of the port administration can construction start. We estimate that Castle

Island and Army Base construction could begin in 1970; Castle Island improve-

ment should be completed in 1971. The Army Base facility could be finished in 1975. The jet planes' departure from Logan to the new airport would

signal the next major step in the redevelopment of the port. This could

occur by 1979, and the enlarged port facility could be in full operation by

the year 1987. A time line of our proposal appears in Figure 6.14.

Should any obstacle bar the course of development projected for

the port facilities, the construction plan can be amended at various decision

points indicated. For example, should the Logan site be unavailable, the

Squantum site would be substituted. Also, if at any time the predicted finan-

cial return fails to materialize, one could halt construction at a minimal loss.

The large degree of flexibility needed for a project of this magnitude was

designed into the construction schedule. The decision points are presented

in Figure 6.15.

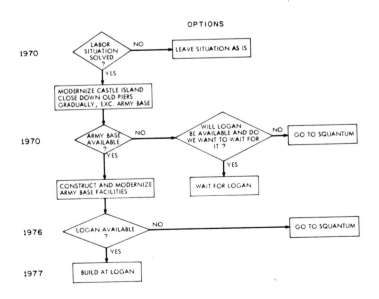

Figure 6.15 Seaport Development Decision Points

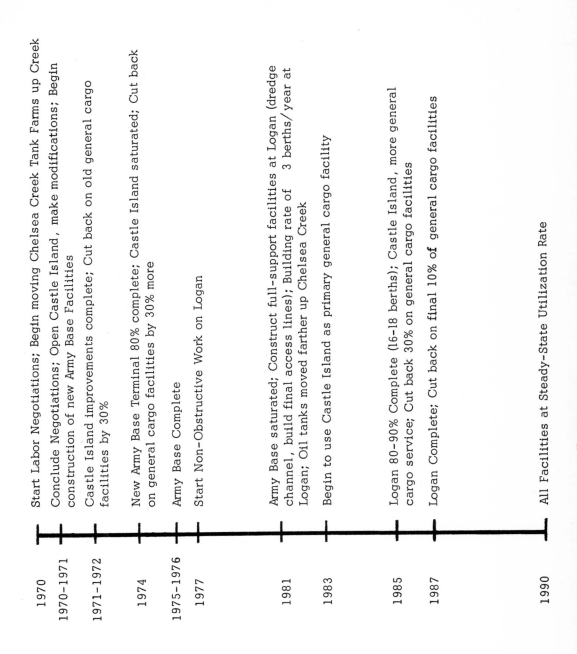

Figure 6.14 Seaport Time Line

In its final form, the new Boston seaport would have facilities at Castle Island for container operations, at the Army Base for general cargo operations, and the majority of activity would be concentrated at the Logan container facility. In addition, the location of a bulk cargo unloading buoy in the Outer Harbor would permit the enhancement of the beauty of the Inner Harbor. Cargo vessels never need travel to the Inner reaches of the Harbor. The three major port facilities will be connected by routes reserved for trucking to the major expressways. In addition, the Logan seaport would share marshalling and storage facilities with the Logan portion of the new airport system. Each of the pieces of this plan coheres to form a design which would attract and accommodate Boston's future market. The specific engineering plans at each particular location are presented in sections 6.10 through 6.15 of this chapter.

Figure 6.16 summarizes predicted demand from the model if this combined alternative is adopted. Note that profits do not rise above the present $1 million level until 1976 because of the cost of constructing new facilities. However, once all the facilities operate and the market expands, profits rise substantially. Likewise, the number of men employed drops to a low of around 100 from 1971 to 1977 before ascending to the ultimate value of 1,250 in 1990. The container berths show a continual climb to a total of 24 while the general cargo berths drop to only 4 in 1977 before rising again and finally leveling off at 8 in the period after 1987. The tonnage shows a continual growth from the present value of less than 1 million tons per year to nearly 7 million in 1990.

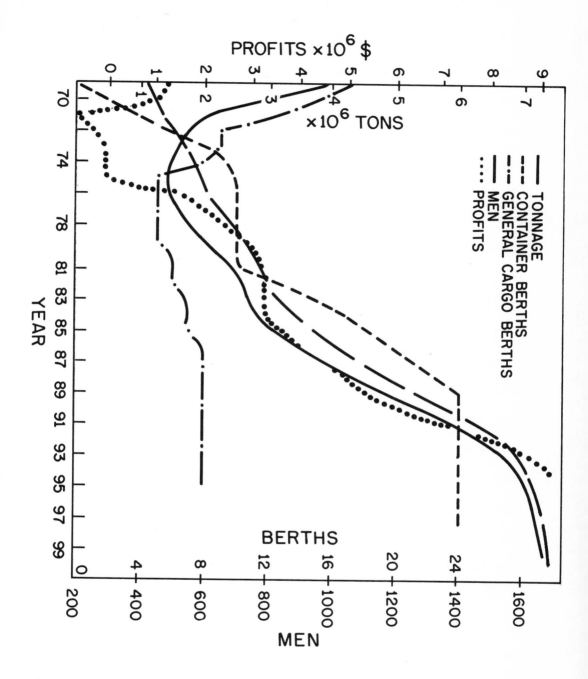

Figure 6.16 Model Prediction of Demand with Combined Alternative

## 6.10   The Physical Facilities

In the discussions offered in preceding sections, we have not delineated the actual equipment and layout at each of the primary port terminals in the new Boston port. The optimum development alternative encourages consideration of many new combinations of facilities. The most general type would include both general cargo and container berths. Each of the primary port locations will house both types of piers during transitional phases of port development. A combination facility can be easily converted into a specialized container terminal if the traffic and labor situations permit and if the optimum development alternative is proceeding according to its time schedule.

Such a combined terminal would look somewhat like that pictured in Figure 6.17. The design includes a very wide apron area, a large storage shed with good truck access, and a very large storage area. Direct truck or boxcar to ship transfer is provided by the dock's transfer cranes, the dock side track, and the pick-up area shown. These transfer cranes are able to transfer truck trailers, containers, or general cargo (Figure 6.18). Two cranes, each of 50 ton capacity, working together can lift all but the heaviest export machinery. A heavy piece of equipment bound for Europe from the General Electric Company plant in Schenectady, New York, for example, would be handled by these cranes. Since the crane operator works out of the port and not out of the ship, it is more logical to have him operate port cranes rather than the ship's gear. It should be noted that the fixed cranes allow continued operation during movement of rail cars on the dock side track. It is an accepted fact that fixed gear is used to greater advantage in this situation than is the

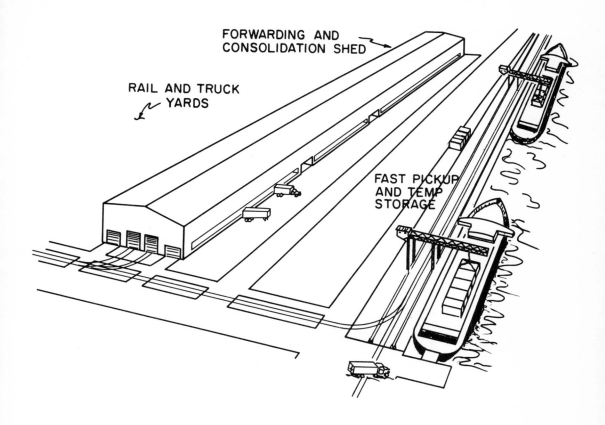

Figure 6.17  Model Seaport Facilities

ship's gear.

The storage shed has two depressed rail tracks and a large amount of truck dock space. This "flush" loading area allows the use of fork lift trucks and similar types of equipment for direct loading of both types of vehicles. Ramps allow the transfer of general cargo directly to the shed from shipside.

All the piers are marginal piers, thereby maximizing the area of the ship adjacent to the dock for unloading purposes and providing easy access to the marshalling area.

The preceding discussion describes typical terminal elements; sections 6.11 through 6.13 will briefly detail the facilities at each of the three major sites of the projected Boston port. Each represents the final configuration of the optimal development alternative. Since such structures would not be completed in the near future, we have made the design general enough to encompass any and all new developments in seaport technology. With the

Figure 6.18 Transfer Cranes

rapid advances in the past few years in unloading techniques and ship design, it is reasonable to assume major changes will present themselves in the future.

6.11    Physical Plan: The Army Base

The Army Base Terminal will occupy but a small space. Consequent disadvantages to be expected during the period of new construction are more than balanced by the Base's usefulness as a land access point to neighboring

Castle Island. Excess demand for the Castle Island facilities and general

cargo berths will be handled at the new Army Base Terminal. Specialized con-

tainer cranes capable of loading or unloading standard 40 foot containers in

less than 2 minutes would be installed at the berths at the eastern end of

the terminal. This is the end furthest from the marshalling yard, but it is

also, due to its size, least adaptable to any other form of cargo handling

facilities. Even if the containers could travel only 20 m.p.h. along the pier,

the containers could be brought to the yard in 3 or 4 minutes, and any con-

tainers bound for local destinations could be picked up right from the ship

or delivered to shipside via truck. Direct rail-to-ship access is also avail-

able although it is harder to deliver containers brought by rail to shipside

in the proper order.

Roll-on roll-off handling of containers will also be used, although at

this time it does not look as though this operation will grow as rapidly as

the lift-on facility. Our design leaves the specific terminal selection to the

planners who can better know the most advantageous method. It is economi-

cally advisable to have 2 cranes per ship. This is true because of the time

differential and the value of ships now being constructed, which is, in turn,

reflected in the high costs of waiting in dock. All together, 5 container cranes

are planned for the Army Base, all of which are capable of handling both

containerized and general cargo. 6 smaller capacity, shore based cranes

are planned for speeding the handling of general breakbulk cargo without the

necessity of using the ship's handling gear. These 3 to 5 ton cranes would

Estimated Costs of Modernizing Army Base: Utilizing Conventional Handling Mea

| | |
|---|---:|
| Foundations and Tracks Container Cranes | $1,000,000 |
| Specialized Container Cranes (5) | 1,250,000 |
| Roll-on, Roll-off Platform | 85,000 |
| Demolition | 200,000 |
| 30 Acres Paved Storage Area, Access Roads | 300,000 |
| Drainage, Lighting, Electric Power, etc. | 150,000 |
| Rebuild Railroad Yards (More Compact) | 400,000 |
| Foundations and Tracks for Gantry Cranes | 1,000,000 |
| High-speed, High-capacity Gantry Cranes (4) | 800,000 |
| High-speed, Low-capacity Cranes (6) | 200,000 |
| Roadway between End Transit Sheds | 15,000 |
| Container Unloading Facility at Marshalling Yard | 100,000 |
| | $5,500,000 |
| Engineering, Financial, Legal, etc. | 750,000 |
| Total | $6,250,000 |

Table 6.9

Costs of Modernizing Army Base: Including Container-Conveyor System

| | |
|---|---:|
| Foundations and Tracks for Container Cranes | $1,000,000 |
| Specialized Container Cranes (5) | 1,250,000 |
| Roll-on, Roll-off Platform | 85,000 |
| Container Conveyor System | 3,000,000 |
| Demolition | 200,000 |
| 30 Acres Paved Storage Area | 300,000 |
| Drainage, Lighting, Electric Power, etc. | 150,000 |
| Railroad Yards Rebuilt (More Compact) | 400,000 |
| High-speed, High-capacity Cranes (4) | 800,000 |
| | $7,185,000 |
| Engineering, Financial, Legal, etc. | 1,065,000 |
| | $8,250,000 |

Table 6.10

greatly improve the handling of general cargo. The larger 20 to 30 ton gantry cranes could be used to handle either large breakbulk items or containers shipped in mixed container-breakbulk cargo ships which will undoubtedly exist for some time.

The 50 foot aprons at the end berths of the terminal are wide enough to allow efficient container handling at the dock, and a return roadway built over one or all of the three railroad tracks running between the transit sheds at the terminal would allow efficient unidirectional traffic on the piers. Six trucks per container crane in operation would be required to keep a smooth flow of traffic.

If called for by future demand, a conveyor system could be implemented for the containers. At this time, an estimated $3 million cannot be justified for this system. Faster ship loading and unloading and other advances in container handling may in the future require such a system.

Table 6.9 presents the estimated costs of upgrading the Army Base Terminal to handle containers by conventional means while Table 6.10 provides an estimate of the cost of upgrading if a complete container-conveyor system were installed.

## 6.12    Physical Plan: Castle Island

To upgrade the facilities at Castle Island is a relatively simple task. The marginal pier can already accommodate container services; furthermore, 1 operational container crane now exists. Our plan requires construction of an additional 3 container cranes and 1 smaller multi-purpose crane. The present marshalling area would need to be improved, but would require no

extensive construction or demolition. The initial costs as presented in
Figure 6.19 are estimated at $6 million. A diagramatic view and a cost
breakdown are also presented in the Figure. Should the development
alternative prove feasible, the second upgrade cycle would begin. This
construction would include storage sheds and a conveyor system at a total
cost of approximately $15 million.

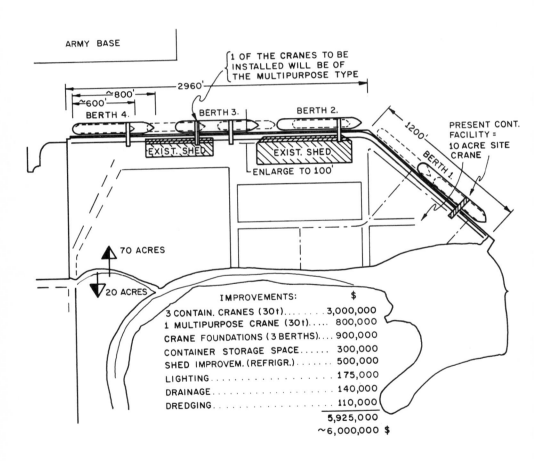

Figure 6.19 Second Castle Island Upgrade Cycle, Stage One

An intricate storage and transportation system for the containers could be instituted as a last phase. This would include a multi-storied storage area, making up for any lack of marshalling area, plus quay container cranes and conveyors to the storage units. These final facilities are presented in Figures 6.20, 6.21 and 6.22.

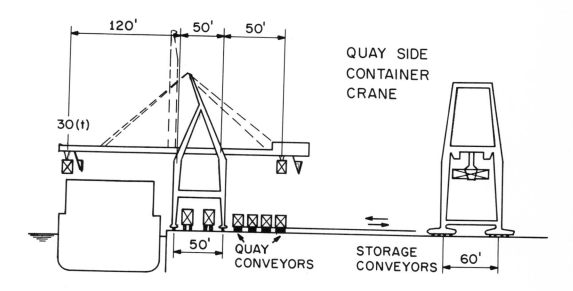

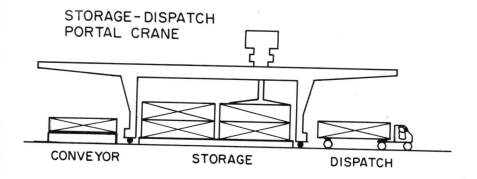

Figure 6.20 Castle Island Facilities

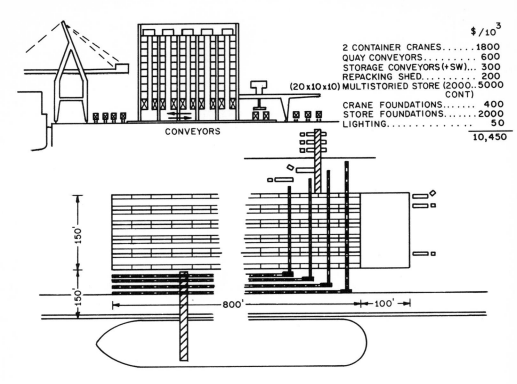

$/10^3$

2 CONTAINER CRANES......1800
QUAY CONVEYORS.........  600
STORAGE CONVEYORS(+SW)... 300
REPACKING SHED..........  200
(20x10x10) MULTISTORIED STORE (2000..5000
CONT)
CRANE FOUNDATIONS.......  400
STORE FOUNDATIONS.......2000
LIGHTING..............   50
                         _____
                         10,450

CONVEYORS

Figure 6.21 Castle Island Conveyor System

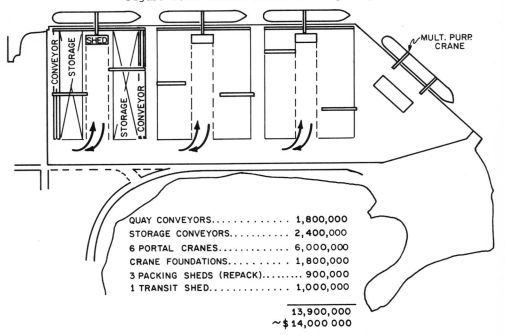

QUAY CONVEYORS............ 1,800,000
STORAGE CONVEYORS.......... 2,400,000
6 PORTAL CRANES............ 6,000,000
CRANE FOUNDATIONS......... 1,800,000
3 PACKING SHEDS (REPACK)........ 900,000
1 TRANSIT SHED............. 1,000,000
                          _____
                          13,900,000
                        ~$ 14,000 000

Figure 6.22 Second Castle Island Upgrade Cycle, Final Stage

## 6.13   Logan Seaport Facility

The proposed seaport facility for Logan should be the finest on the

East Coast. It will have excellent access both from the sea and from land.

It will be located on the existing channel into Boston. The expressways

presently serving the airport will accommodate direct truck service to the

docks.

20 berths will be built on the southern edge of the airport site. They

will occupy approximately 200 acres of existing land and 160 acres of filled

land (Figure 6.23). All piers will be of the marginal type for easy access

from sea and land. A new channel as shown in this Figure will allow ships

to enter and leave 13 of the 20 berths without having to turn around in a

narrow channel. Delay and time consuming tugboat maneuvering will there-

by be substantially reduced.

The plan is presented in five stages, allowing new berths to be built

in groups of approximately 4 as needed. Phase I can be started while Logan

is still operating as a full scale jet-port; the remaining phases must wait

until Logan has been converted to a V/STOL port. The port will by no means

be confined to 20 berths. One obvious area for expansion is the Bird Island

Flats area which could be filled to create space for 10 to 15 additional berths.

Table 6.11 indicates that the expected average cost per berth is

$1.5 million. Some variation will occur from berth to berth; for example,

an $85,000 roll-on roll-off ramp sometimes may be substituted for the $250,000

crane. However, since the facility is expected to handle primarily lift-off

containers, the preliminary design may best assume a constant cost of

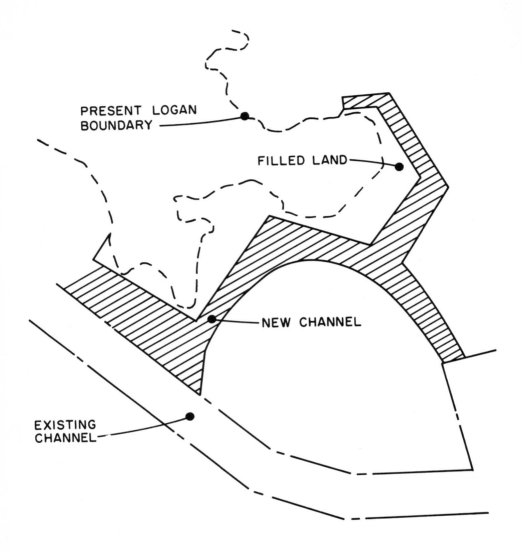

Figure 6.23 Logan Seaport Facility

$1.5 million per berth. The locations of the berths and the channel to be dredged are shown in Figure 6.24.

Table 6.12 shows the sequential development of the port. The land purchase in the preliminary stage is based on 200 acres at $3 per square foot.

Cost per Berth

| | |
|---|---:|
| Bulkhead (750 feet at $1000/ft) | $750,000 |
| Apron and crane track (750 feet at $400/ft) | 300,000 |
| Crane | 250,000 |
| Paved Upland (12 acres at $10,000/acre) | 120,000 |
| Storm Drains (12 acres at $3,000/acre) | 36,000 |
| Lighting (12 acres at $2,000/acre) | 24,000 |
| Total | $1,480,000 |

Table 6.11 Logan Seaport Cost per Berth

The sale is merely a formality since the Massachusetts Port Authority owns both the airport and the seaports and needs only to transfer the land internally.

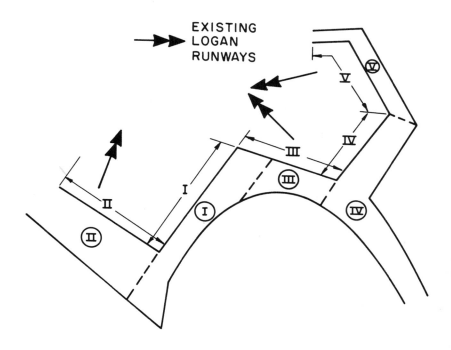

Figure 6.24 Berth Locations and New Channel

|  | | Cost in Millions of $ | Cumulative Total |
|---|---|---|---|
| **Preliminary** | | | |
| Land (Transfer within Port Authority) | | 26.0 | |
| Engineering, Financial, Legal | | 5.0 | |
| | Total | 31.0 | 31.0 |
| **Phase I** | | | |
| Dredge and Fill | | 3.00 | |
| 5 Berths | | 7.50 | |
| Railroad Holding Yard and Spur | | 0.25 | |
| Road Lining | | 0.25 | |
| Container Packing Shed | | 0.50 | |
| | Total | 11.50 | 42.5 |
| **Phase II** | | | |
| Dredge and Fill | | 0.50 | |
| 4 Berths | | 6.00 | |
| Shed | | 1.50 | |
| | Total | 8.0 | 50.5 |
| **Phase III** | | | |
| Dredge and Fill | | 1.50 | |
| 4 Berths | | 6.00 | |
| Container Packing Shed | | 0.50 | |
| Railroad Yard and Spur | | 0.25 | |
| Road Work | | 0.25 | |
| | Total | 8.5 | 59.0 |
| **Phase IV** | | | |
| Dredge and Fill | | 3.0 | |
| 3 Berths | | 4.5 | |
| Shed | | 1.5 | |
| | Total | 9.0 | 68.0 |
| **Phase V** | | | |
| Dredge and Fill | | 2.0 | |
| 4 Berths | | 6.0 | |
| | Total | 8.0 | 76.0 |

Table 6.12 Sequential Development of the Port

The $5 million engineering, financial, and legal fund is intended to cover the design and construction of the entire 20 berth area. Not all of this sum will be spent before construction begins.

The land required for a containerized berth may be broken into two parts: the marshalling yard or container storage area and supporting facilities.

The area required for the latter versus the number of contiguous berths is

shown in Figure 6.25.

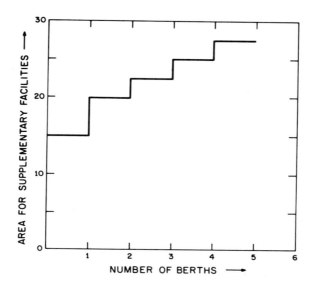

Figure 6.25 Area for Supplementary Facilities as a Function of Number of Berths

Supporting facilities include:

    Roads and truck maneuvering area
    Rail spur and holding yard
    Administration and control building
    Parking lot
    Container repacking shed
    Maintenance and repair facilities
    Refrigerator yard

The non-linearity of Figure 6.25 reflects the inefficiency of having separate

support facilities for each berth. The exact number of berths that can be

served by a single support facility, such as a container repacking shed, is

a function of the layout of the port and tonnage handled. For a typical design a separate set of support facilities, excluding the administrative

area, will be required for each set of 4 or 5 berths. In other words, about

6 acres of supporting facilities are required per berth for a well designed

port.

The most important and largest land requirement for a container berth

is the marshalling yard. The storage provided must be sufficient for about

one and one half times the capacity of the average ship calling at the berth;

that is about enough storage for 1,100 containers where the average ship

carries 720 containers. Although there will usually be containers from 4 or

5 ships in the yard at once, a large percentage of the containers will be off-

loaded from the ship directly to rail cars or highway trucks and will never need

to be stored.

The best location for the storage yard is immediately behind the berth.

The land required varies with the type of storage. At least four methods are

possible. The automated equipment needed for alternative four would cost at

| Storage | Yard Vehicle | Stack Height (No. of containers) | Area for 1,100 Containers |
|---|---|---|---|
| 1. Truck Chassis | Tractor | 1 | 12 acres |
| 2. Ground | Saddle Trucks | 2 | 6 acres |
| 3. Ground | Yard Crane, Tractor Trailor | 4 | 3 acres |
| 4. Multi-Level | Automated | 10 | 1 acre |

least $15 million. Trading off 11 acres with $15 million, the cost of land

would have to be $32 per square foot. Therefore, multi-level storage is not

a serious contender at present. Similarly, in alternative three, the cranes

and tracks needed to allow movement throughout the yard would cost several

million dollars. Land would have to cost about $10 per square foot to make
alternative three viable.

One cannot choose so easily between alternatives one and two. Straddle
trucks are only slightly more expensive than yard tractors. In first cost terms,
the straddle trucks are cheaper than an additional 6 acres at typical land prices
of $1 to $3 per square foot. However, use of the straddle trucks requires an
additional transfer of the container. When chassis storage is used, the highway
tractor can drive into the yard and leave the container in a prescribed spot with
additional equipment required. When straddle trucks are used, every container
must be lifted off the highway trailer. Figure 6.26 compares the increased operating cost associated with operation in a 6 acre yard ($1.50 per lift) with the
cost of the additional area required to handle up to 1,100 containers per acre
using truck chassis storage. Here, a capital recovery factor of 0.06 has been
used, as can be seen, for the assumptions stated that the operating costs associated with the smaller area override the land costs for volumes over 600 containers per week. Therefore, chassis storage is recommended.

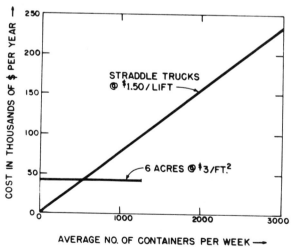

Figure 6.26 Differential Operating Costs and
Land Costs for Two Types of Marshalling Yards

Automatic ship docking does not appear feasible for Boston at this time. The cost of tugboat hire is very small when compared to ship waiting time cost of about $150 per hour. Therefore, the major trade-off in justifying an automated system is between the cost of the system and the ship hours saved. When good access is provided to marginal piers, as in the proposed Logan seaport, a ship can sail very close to the docking area under its own power. The time required for a tug to maneuver the ship the last few hundred feet into the berth is virtually negligible. Good access is cheaper than automatic ship docking and accomplishes the same purpose.

In considering multiple cranes to off-load a single container ship, the savings of the ship's waiting time again dominates other savings such as increased berth utilization. A container crane can be amortized for about $12,500 per year. Assuming a shipper would pay $75 to the port to save an hour of ship waiting time, a berth would have to save about 167 ship hours per year or 3.2 hours a week. Assuming 2 ships per week, Figure 6.27 shows that an average of at least 100 containers per ship would have to be off-loaded to justify 2 cranes per berth. The use of 3 cranes was not considered because it would be impossible to get enough trucks on the apron to service them all. In practice, if there are several contiguous berths, the cranes can be rolled along their tracks to gang 2 on a single ship. There will usually be free cranes for this purpose, since berths are only used about 50% of the available time.

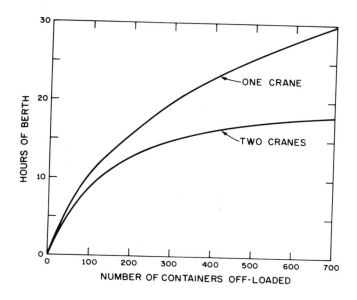

Figure 6.27 Crane Demand as dictated by Berth Use

## 6.14    Liquid Bulk Facilities

There seems to be little reason to require that an oil tanker steam all the way up Chelsea River only to be pumped out. Such a trip interferes with air traffic in 3 of the 4 Logan runways, and consumes much valuable time. Savings in ship time result from an off-shore oil facility as does elimination of that portion of the traffic problem. As to pollution, ballast need not be pumped out in Boston, and the lesser incidental oil spillage is subject to the planner's control.

With the construction of a low cost pipeline from a location at Logan Airport to the unloading buoys in the Outer Harbor, tankers may be

unloaded at that location thereby saving a trip to the Inner Harbor. This
feature has the added advantage of shortening the distance and therefore
the time between the shipping lanes and the unloading facility, consequently lowering the cost of the trip and of the final product. In addition, the
location of unloading facilities in the Outer Harbor would allow large supertankers to call at the Port of Boston without fear of delay or danger to the
ship navigating narrow passages in the harbor.

## 6.15    Dry Bulk Facilities

The East Boston grain facilities seem to be adequate and efficient.
They were built for rail service (as was the rest of the port), but since railroads still handle almost all of the grain, no serious disadvantage exists
here. In fact, the only serious current problem stems from the facility's
location.

Ships bound to and from East Boston travel up Presidents' Roads,
passing by Logan Airport. Certain runways cannot be used while ships pass
due to the height of modern ship superstructures. Coexistence, thanks to
communication between airport and seaport offices, can continue but the
hazards inherent in this situation could be avoided by changing the location
of dry bulk facilities.

## 6.16    New Techniques

In the previous sections, new technological developments in seaborne
transportation and terminal facilities were but briefly mentioned. One of the
ideas considered deserves note in this report.

A ship's time is spent traveling from port to port, boarding small or large amounts of cargo at each port, and then, after the voyage, delivering this cargo to its various destinations. Enormous new ships lessen the likelihood that an entire shipload of cargo from one port would be destined for another single port, thereby permitting a direct, time-saving voyage. A possible solution to this problem might be seagoing barges, which would load at different locations, meet at sea, sort out cargo as to destination, and separate when reaching the coast to deliver and again pick up new cargo. Although this concept is still in the seminal stage, study is being conducted in the Maritime Administration Research Program of the Department of Naval Architecture at M.I.T. This program's version of such seagoing barges and appropriate unloading techniques are presented in Figures 6.28 and 6.29. We believe that many innovations shall be seen in the field of seaborne technology.

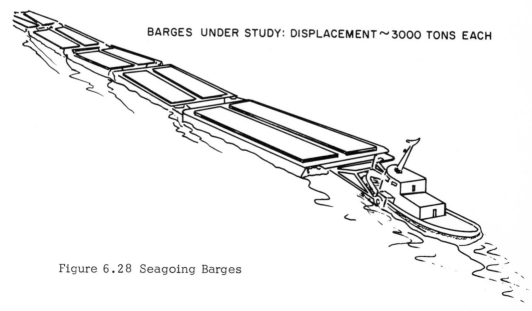

BARGES UNDER STUDY: DISPLACEMENT ~ 3000 TONS EACH

Figure 6.28 Seagoing Barges

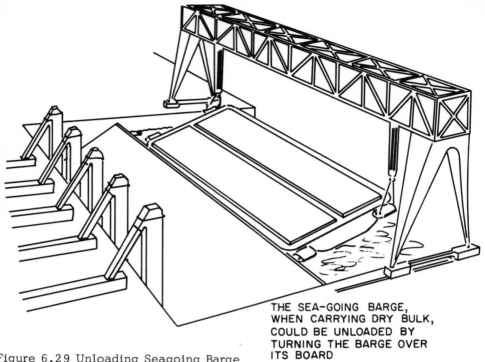

Figure 6.29 Unloading Seagoing Barge

THE SEA-GOING BARGE,
WHEN CARRYING DRY BULK,
COULD BE UNLOADED BY
TURNING THE BARGE OVER
ITS BOARD

6.17    The Second Design Alternative

Although the optimum design alternative seems by far the best course
to follow, there remains one other major alternative: a deliberate phasing
out of all port operations with the exception of the liquid and dry bulk facilities
outlined in sections 6.14 and 6.15 in this chapter. Although Boston and New
England shippers would be obliged to find alternate route of cargo transport,
Boston could reap distinctly postive benefits from new functions located in
the harbor. By eliminating the majority of Boston Harbor shipping and by
controlling most of the shoreline, the City of Boston could develop the Harbor
as an integrated community resource.

A bill providing funds for the state to buy all the Harbor Islands should pass the 1970 session of the legislature. These islands and the shore land presently used by the port would lend themselves to varying uses, including large recreation areas, complexes, such as a university campus, which would serve the community, and urban housing. Boston possesses one of the finest harbors in the world; if it is not to be utilized for a compact, efficient, modern, pollution-free seaport, then it should house such living and service areas.

It should be pointed out that a harbor airport would not necessarily interfere with use of the Harbor as a community area. Also, specialty port operations and contractual deliveries from operators directly to consumers would be permitted since they would involve only the limited remaining private piers.

Once the seaport had been finally voted into oblivion, the Harbor region could be placed under the jurisdiction of a regional governmental agency which would use the Harbor so as to best alleviate Boston's urban needs. Obviously, this alternative as well would require comprehensive planning.

## 6.18   Summary

We used a straightforward procedure to determine the best direction for development of the Port of Boston in the future. We assumed first that lower total costs will attract more trade to a port and will increase the total market of the port. That recent developments in seaport technology can be significant in lowering the cost of port operation is a further assumption.

Alternatives were then generated and a decision procedure for choosing the
best alternative was constructed. Finally the options and particular designs
were explored.

Our primary assumption was that a shipper decides his routing on the
basis of lowest port cost. Figure 6.30 presents the elements in total trip
cost. Figure 6.31 presents an example of the procedure used to determine

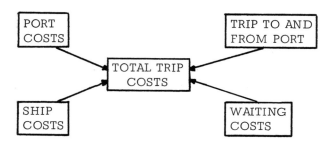

Figure 6.30 Elements in Total Trip Cost

the size of the new market compared with the cost reduction achieved. In
this example, it was determined that a shipper would incur an additional cost
of $8.10 if he shipped through Boston rather than New York. After many such
comparisons we mapped Boston's potential market. By summing the possible
cargo volumes which might be obtained from each of the major areas it is
possible to determine the potential market size as a function of the total cost.
If the port costs in Boston are lowered $15/ton the volume shipped through
Boston would rise an expected 13 million tons per year.

Much of the desired technology has already been developed. Contain-

|              | Buffalo Boston Europe | Buffalo New York Europe |
|--------------|-----------------------|-------------------------|
| Truck        | $21.80/TON            | $20.00/TON              |
| Port Costs   | 23.10/TON             | 16.50/TON               |
| Water Costs  | 7.00/TON              | 7.30/TON                |
| Total        | $51.90/TON            | $43.80/TON              |

Figure 6.31 Typical Cost Reduction Needed to Attract New Market

erization can reduce port handling costs by as much as 90% or $10-$12/ton.

A dynamic system model relating the various sectors of the seaport was created to help evaluate the Boston port economic situation. This model uses the concepts of information feedback theory and suggests how the port will grow or decline with the policy decisions made. The inputs to the system are the potential demand as a function of tonnage, and the present costs, tonnages, facilities, and men employed. The outputs are in terms of new tonnage, facilities, costs, men employed, and profits to the port administration.

The model was used as a tool in evaluating various development alternatives. The results of this comparison were shown in Figure 5.21. The costs of constructing the optimal alternative were then found and a development plan was formulated. It projected the use of Castle Island, the Army Base, and 200 acres at Logan.

In its final form after 1990 such a seaport would return a profit of $9.3 million to the port management authority and employ 1,350 men handling 5.6 million tons of cargo per year. The proposed time schedule has been summarized in a time line, Figure 6.19.

In addition to improvements in the general cargo port in Boston,
certain recommendations were made concerning bulk facilities in the port
and over-all port policies. We urged the removal of bulk liquid unloading
facilities from the inner harbor to mooring buoys in the outer harbor. In
addition, whatever the condition of the seaport and whatever the status
of a proposal such as ours, consolidated facilities will use harbor resources
more efficiently. Modern cargo handling procedures need a smaller area,
fewer men, and cost less than the traditional methods in use in Boston.
However, the efficient activity resulting from implementation of a comprehensive plan will demand increasing numbers of workers and expanded
facilities as it brings about a larger market and consequent profit to
management.

The problem is finally an investment dilemma. If the risks are
too great, then one must choose to retire Boston altogether from the seaport
industry rather than continue to deprive the citizens of the region of a
significant resource.

Chapter 7

PORT LABOR


The excellence of the BOSPORUS design avails nothing, its proposal is absurd, if it is not acceptable to labor unions whose opposition would have the power to veto its construction or cripple its operation. To learn the role organized labor could be expected to play in the implementation of any plan for new port facilities or policies, we undertook an extensive study of the current situation in the Port of Boston. We hoped to subsequently invent methods to surmount probable obstacles in this area. The obligation of those responsible for the management of the Port of Boston to promote social good as well as efficient operation further impels inquiry into the relationship between new facilities and policies and the labor force.

Two basic issues have proved to be the main impediments to congenial labor-management relations. Wage disputes, the prime and historical source of controversy, spring from the dilemma of providing adequate and reasonable income levels to individual laborers while minimizing employer costs. The rising cost of living, a universal plague to all capital-labor relations, cannot be controlled by the operators. Wage rates therefore have been delegated to the judgment of managers and union leaders. The

bugaboo of automation provides the second field of battle. In this case

labor's goal of maximum employment is incompatible with management's

desire to trim costs by adopting new production technologies. Where

management ignores this conflict and innovates, labor's successful adher-

ence to its goal appears as featherbedding.

Our task presents two facets: first, we must employ the labor

force at a level of efficiency which will ensure economic use of valuable

port equipment; equally, we must satisfy the needs of the Boston longshore-

men so that the labor unions will accept our proposals.

## 7.1    Airport Labor

The realization of improvements in air facilities and operation has

apparently never been impeded seriously by labor difficulties. There appear

two probable reasons. First, rapid and continuous expansion in trade volume

have provided income and employment levels to reasonably satisfy everyone

concerned; even those workers discontented with their present jobs can look

forward to almost certain improvement. Second, the unusually fast pace

of technological innovation in the industry has had the effect of institution-

alizing the process of change. Airline employees have become accustomed

to adjusting to successive new methods. These favorable situations have

combined to provide relative peace in the airline industry.

Clearly this is not to say that disputes do not occur. The past

three years have seen two major airline employees' strikes. The first was

a ten day strike against Pan American Airlines by the Air Line Pilots'
Association in August 1965, the issue at hand being the maximum continuous time which an airplane crew should be expected to work. The second
and better known disagreement resulted in the month and one half long
strike in the summer of 1966 by the International Association of Machinists
and Aerospace Workers against all the major United States carriers. This
conflict was solely over wages. These two incidents did not relate to
technological change, and they did not stem from any long standing griev-
ances over principle; rather, narrow and immediate issues were at their
genesis. In sum, they typify the kind of labor dispute with which this
study does not concern itself, since it represents no direct threat to air
transport mutability.

In a new airport design only the baggage-handling function might
experience a reluctant acceptance. Projections aspire ultimately to eliminate all human baggage handlers in normal operation. Several airlines,
however, have been rapidly automating their baggage services, so far
with no incidence of labor difficulty. In any event, the redcaps enjoy
only small economic power. This aspect, therefore, fails to sway our
conclusion that no serious objections to airport innovation appear likely
from the labor sector.

## 7.2    Seaport Labor: History

The longshoring industry, both in general and at the Boston port
in particular, claims a long history of poor labor-management relations.

The organized labor force entered Boston history in 1912 with a profitless

wage strike by 2300 longshoremen. As a result of this reverse, the

Knights of Labor were discredited as the mens' bargaining agent and were

supplanted by the International Longshoremens' Association (ILA). The

longshoremen then temporarily abandoned port-wide strikes and relied

instead on pier level stoppage as a means to improved conditions.

Formal peace, with widespread informal accord over such issues

as work rules, "quickie" strikes, and labor conditions, held until 1931.

Then, employee attempts to extort reformation of labor practices by a two

month strike ended in thorough defeat. Although the workers maintained

good discipline, the shippers employed strikebreakers to force the men to

authorize the International president, Joseph P. Ryan, to bargain for an

agreement. The episode embittered the Boston locals against Ryan who,

they felt, had sold them out.

During the next five years, a series of unsatisfactory and short-

lived contracts were drawn. From 1935 to 1950 no contract could be

negotiated, and work was performed under the terms prevailing in New

York. The longshoremen continued to go out on wildcat strikes to attain

particular demands, and, because of the nature of shipping economics,

these tactics usually triumphed.

Yet in the late forties, labor relations improved for several reasons.

Increased public awareness of union practices and the existence of employer

sponsored welfare funds gave the ILA a stake in speedy, mutually acceptable

settlements. The formation of the Boston Shipping Association (BSA) in

1946, and the active interest of offices of the Federal Mediation and
Conciliation Service and the Boston Port Authority advanced communication.
In 1950, a contract was negotiated which resembled the 1935 arrangement
but incorporated some revisions in the areas of meal hours and fringe
benefits. Work stoppages on loaded piers, however, continued to under-
mine harmonious cooperation.

1954 marked the emergence of a new, more rational management
attitude toward labor. Prior to that date, shippers had bargained from
the principle that labor union demands should be fought to the limit since
any concessions would open the way for a union takeover of port operation.
After the Korean War, employers somehow came to realize that many union
claims were valid and could be equitably granted. This opinion was com-
prehended in the contract in 1954 which instituted the first workable
grievance procedure in Boston longshoring history. Fourteen years of
evidence shows that a grievance procedure has substantially limited the
number of "quickie" strikes; it owes its effectiveness largely to the conscientious action of both the BSA and the ILA.

Although many differences have found settlements, among them
the hiring hall agreement of 1966 and a 1969 agreement to allow containerization in exchange for a guaranteed amount of work each year, a
pattern of noncooperativeness persists that seems to have two historical
roots. One is the birth of longshore unions in an era of rampant laissez-
faire capitalism, a time when unions were widely considered and heartily
hated as illegitimate offspring of the American Bill of Rights. Organized

labor was obliged to assert its simple right to exist until World War II
with the sequel that, even today, the men feel bitter toward shipping
management. The second source is the antiquity of the shipping industry,
the nature of whose work has evolved little until very recently. Work
practices and patterns of responsibility have stiffened over a long period,
creating a traditionalism on the part of both labor and management equaled
in few industries. This petrification provides instant problems for anyone
essaying to renovate cargo handling methods.

7.3     Seaport Labor: Problems

The Boston longshore industry embraces three major interest groups:
shipping companies, stevedoring companies, and longshoremen (including
clerks, etc.) The shipping concerns contract with the stevedoring companies for work to be done on a yearly or a ship by ship basis. The
stevedoring firms then hire the longshoremen as needed. Contracts are
negotiated between the BSA and the ILA, which represent respectively the
carriers and the stevedores. Prior to April 1969 no formal agreement had
been drawn between the ILA and BSA since 1962; wages had been set at
the level stipulated in the New York contract. In April Boston stevedores
agreed to a three year contract covering wages, hours, pensions, and use
of containerized facilities. Though the current New York and Boston contracts make Boston's prices lower than those of New York, local habits
make Boston, financially and generally, a less attractive port.

In the recent past, Labor's resistance to management's goal of efficiency and modern operation had been most evident in the areas of work rules and work habits. Since the 1969 contract, work restrictions have been largely lifted. Sling load limits are now set by management according to standards of safety. The standard gang size has fallen from 22 to 20 men. More essentially, the ILA has agreed to handle containerized shipments and to accept palletization. Theoretically, port operations should be predictable and efficient. The above discussion, however, neglects the men who are to work in accordance with the rules; the longshoremen continue to display their characteristically notorious working habits. The Boston longshoreman is traditionally an independent soul. Gangs of unspecified number report for work late, short of men, or both. Frequently, a gang will leave its assigned ship without permission in order to work on a job which promises to last longer; similarly, the men tend to leave their ship before completion of the job. Another headache is the "quickie" strike, an unauthorized walkout affecting a single ship, usually over an issue such as the class of cargo and the possibility for extra pay. These unruly actions to a greater or lesser extent cancel the carefully worked out specifications for port operation set down in the 1969 contract.

Secondary circumstances aggravate this problem. The high average age of the workers (about 58) tends to make them more mindful of their own short-term interests than of the port's future welfare. The vast majority of the men come from a Boston Irish background, and their ethnic homogen-

eity precludes national rivalry, a psychological spur to competitive performance. Finally, the longshoremen esteem the prerogative to pick and
choose their hours and the amount of work performed; it has been affirmed
that they prefer this freedom to the guarantee of a regular wage, despite
union demands which have implied that a guaranteed number of hours is
primarily desirable. But union members are undisciplined to the extent
that they have refused to honor contracts signed by their own representatives and accepted by vote of the membership. The union leadership,
fearful of jeopardizing its power by alienating its constituents, look
with disfavor on proposals which would reduce the number of longshoremen employed.

Prior to 1969, attempts had been made to dispatch the wellsprings
of inefficiency listed above. In 1966, an agreement was negotiated between
the ILA and the BSA which replaced the old "shape up" hiring system in
which each employer would designate a hiring boss who would select
workers individually with a central hiring hall. The union agreed to maintain thirty permanent gangs of 22 men each and to cooperate with the BSA's
automation. In return, the longshoremen were guaranteed 1600 hours of pay
per year. This compact was expected to end vitually all of the above
problems. But, appartently, the lack of discipline among the men combined
with the incoherence of the newly arranged gangs to yield equally low or
lower labor productivity than before. Whether, despite the 1969 bid for
operational agreement which was achieved on paper, the reality of efficient
operation will continue to elude the Boston Port remains to be seen.

## 7.4    Labor: Prospects

At present an agreement to automate port operations in Boston has been reached. Containers are being handled with the use of ship's gear and palletization is permitted. However, cooperation with this degree of automation was only achieved by accession to the ILA's demand for 2,080 hours of work per year at more than double the previous hourly wage. Labor made these demands to off-set the shrinkage of work hours which accompanies containerized operation. The natural savings shippers enjoy due to automation are thereby reduced by the total amount of this guaranteed annual wage. Clearly, the optimum solution to this labor-management conflict is yet to be found.

Circumstances seem to conspire overwhelmingly against labor solutions, but in fact one may posit considerable gounds for hope. Forces exist which may tend to propitiate the unions toward automation without featherbedding. Chief among these is the fact that the men are very apt to lose their jobs through the simple demise of Boston's trade. Further cause to hope lies in the fact that the union leadership headed by International Vice-President John F. Moran displays conscientious  sincere interest in the men's welfare, and basic reason in negotiations after one discounts the normal amount of public posturing. In association these two elements - the threat of complete work loss and wise leadership - promoted the West Coast Mechanization and Modernization Agreement in 1960 and should presumably be instrumental in advancing constructive solutions for Boston as well.

Finally, to culminate in success, automation must be prefigured by management's progress from a rational to a practical view toward the longshoremen. On the West Coast, the Pacific Maritime Association recognized that the men had a vested interest in their jobs which could be bought by management for a reasonable price. From this point of view, it is obvious that employers can convince the men to give up their job rights by making it worth their while to sell. Traditional managers may balk at such philosophy, but they cannot deny that it produces results, as attested by the West Coast longshoremen's agreement. The merit of this approach for Boston emerges as one imagines how one could thereby deal with many of the local labor problems listed above. For instance, by making profits accrue to longshoremen who quit the industry, the men's often deplored preoccupation with their own short term gain could be turned to the advantage of the port management, which would reap subsequent long term benefits. Furthermore, if the men can individually perceive that their own interest lies in such a settlement, the burden of persuasion and discipline would be removed from the shoulders of the union leadership.

To summarize, a modernization scheme for the Boston seaport appears viable so long as administrators recognize the rights of the longshoremen to their jobs or to monetary compensation. A final argument for negotiating on this basis: while all else has failed, this approach has never been tried.

## 7.5     Plans for Solution

We will plan to automate assuming that unnecessary laborers will be phased out of port operations in return for money. Give this premise, we may choose among several designs; therefore, we will conjointly develop comparisons based on their costs of implementation and their benefits expressed in reduction of labor costs per ton of cargo. For a desired drop in per ton labor cost from $c_1'$, present labor cost-ton for all labor, to $c_2$, the desired cost/ton for union labor (see Figure 7.1),

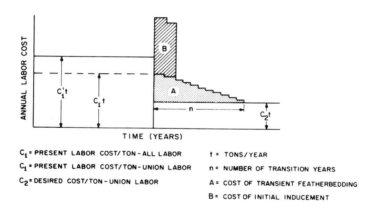

Figure 7.1 Transitional Labor Costs

several steps must be taken. First, all non-union labor can be dismissed at no cost to management whatever, thereby reducing the cost per ton to a level $c_1$. Two costs are then associated with phasing out union members. First, one must pay the excess labor force during the transition period between $c_1$ and $c_2$. Second, management must pay the men (or the union)

to induce them to accept the plan is the first place. For a given proposal,

these costs can be plotted in terms of the associated improvements in

labor rates, $c_2/c_1$. The four plans which have been analyzed are described

below. Calculations were based on the numbers give in Table 7.1.

Table 7.1

Relevant Labor and Cost Statistics
for the Port of Boston

| | |
|---|---|
| Number of ILA Longshoremen | 1000 |
| Number of ILA Longshoremen who work full-time | 700 |
| Number of Part-Time Longshoremen | 300 |
| Number of ILA Clerks, etc. | 200 |
| Number of Part-Time Clerks, etc. | 35 |
| | |
| Longshoremen's Pay: | |
| Straight Wages | $3.62/hr |
| Benefits | $1.31/hr |
| Clerks' Wages | $30/day |
| | |
| Average Longshoremen's Age | 58 |
| | |
| Estimated Labor Productivity: | |
| Break-Bulk | 12 tons/gang-hr |
| Containerized | 180 tons/gang-hr |
| | |
| Cost of General Cargo Handling due to all longshoring | $8.00/ton |
| Cost due to all Checking, etc. | $4.00/ton |
| Total Cost due to all Labor ($c_1'$) | $12.00/ton |
| Cost if only Union Labor were employed ($c_1$) | $8.50/ton |
| | |
| Total Annual Cargo Throughput | $1.1 \times 10^6$ tons |

The first alternative is natural attrition. The Boston longshore labor force currently declines at a rate of about thirty men per year. Since the average age of the men is rising, one may assume a higher rate in time. In an estimated fifteen years, therefore, effectively all the present longshoremen will have retired, giving $c_2/c_1 = 0$. No inducement cost attends this solution which simply recognizes the extension of a present condition. The cost of paying superfluous laborers for an average of eleven years, however, would be high.

The second plan is to offer a lump payoff. It would, in all likelihood, be possible to provide the immediate retirement of any desired number of men simply by granting them their predicted life's earnings. The average 58 year old longshoreman would find himself substantially amenable to retirement when offered $50,000. The advantage of this settelement's immediate effect would be qualified, of course, by its very high short-term cost.

A mandatory early retirement plan would resemble the West Coast Mechanization and Modernization Agreement. It would oblige automatic retirement at a relatively early age in exchange for an exceptionally high pension. For the purpose of present calculations, the retirement age has been set at 62, with a pension of $300 per month until age 65 at which time the pension falls to its current level of about $150 per month. One could conceivably vary the retirement age to provide for faster or slower workforce reduction as desired.

A fourth possibility is the semi-retirement plan. Many men feel themselves well able to work past age 62 (or 65) and would want to earn a supplemental income; moreover, as stated earlier, a number actually

prefer to dictate their own work level rather than to be bound to a

regular, guaranteed income and mandatory retirement at a certain age.

Nothing bars the incorporation of this preference into a retirement scheme.

A sample plan would call for the men to "semi-retire" at age 62 with a

guaranteed pension of $230 per month until age 67. They would enjoy

the option, however, of working up to eight hours a week at regular

wages, thus earning an additional $1540 per year. This plan is depicted

in Figure 7.2. The longshoreman's love of independence in choosing

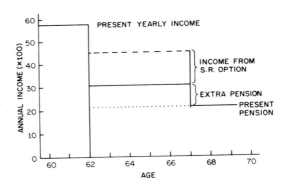

Figure 7.2 The Semi-Retirement Plan

The four plans outlined above are compared in Figure 7.3. This

graph shows the cost of solving the labor problem as a function of the

reduction in labor cost ($c_2/c_1$) due to automation. Obviously, each

alternative plan becomes more expensive as the labor requirement per

ton declines. A labor reduction ratio from 1.0 down to 0.22 under the

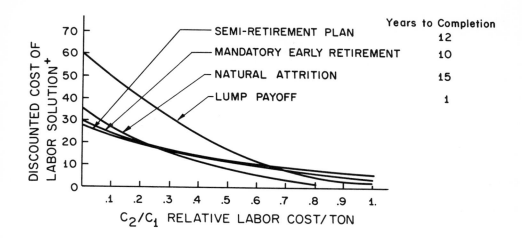

Figure 7.3 Labor Plans

natural attrition program incurs the lowest cost. In manpower, one would

be spared expense for three of the four mean required presently. (This

ratio would rise if one used a lower interest rate for the present value

calculations, reaching 0.35 for a 0% interest rate.) However, since the

attrition plan does not involve the union's active consent, future ob-

stacles may lie in ambush. For more drastic reductions in labor below

0.22, one of the two retirement plans would be preferable.

From experience, one may predict that containerized operation

will cut labor costs per ton to 1/6 of their break bulk level. If full

automation and computerized scheduling go into effect, the cost ratio

$c_2/c_1$ could be expected to reach as low as 0.1 or 0.05. In this context, an accelerated retirement scheme would be desirable. Given personnel preferences discussed above, the semi-retirement plan appears most fruitful.

It should be noted that in all of the above analyses, we have inferred tonnage through the port to be constant. In fact, the introduction of containerization would stimulate growth in the volume of trade and, given a fixed labor force, would cut the labor cost per ton. Our figures are therefore conservative.

## 7.6    Labor Recommendations

The semi-retirement plan in all probability would be the proposal most acceptable to labor. It would stand as the backbone of any offer made by the new port management to the ILA. Rejection by union leaders, whose positions would eventually be nullified by the mens' resignations, could be spared by the gift of new power; for example, one could appoint the International Vice-President a member of the new Metropolitan Port Commission. An influential position on this policy-making management body would greatly enhance his prestige among his members and peers in the International organization.

As additional provisions, a contract might propose scholarships or training programs for descendants of longshoremen and perhaps a stock distribution plan, the latter to further lure the men to early retirement by affording them a chance to benefit from shippers' swelled profits.

As the above discussion suggests, it appears that a willing consent to and continued abidence by an agreement to automate could be won from

the Boston longshore industry if a combination of constructive proposals

were offered by the port management.

Chapter **8**

PORT MANAGEMENT AND FINANCE

An aura of mystery seems to surround all government associated agencies and management structures; certainly in the areas of funding, bonds, or financing they are regarded with considerable suspicion by everyone save officionados and economists. Yet natural aversion cannot deter us from their study, for financing must be incorporated into plans for a new port.

To begin, we considered the various functions our management organization would be called on to perform. Our task was then to design a structure that would be efficient and yet subservient to the interest groups directly involved. We found such a structure indeed feasible and subject to public control (Figure 8.1). Our funding scheme follows, with minor variations, accepted patterns of capitalization, and conforms to both legal and governmental restrictions. Moreover, with time, both managerial expenses and retirement bonds can be absorbed by the profits of the port.

8.1    Present Port Management

The agency directly responsible for port operation - both of the airport and seaport - is the Massachusetts Port Authority. A logical first questio

254

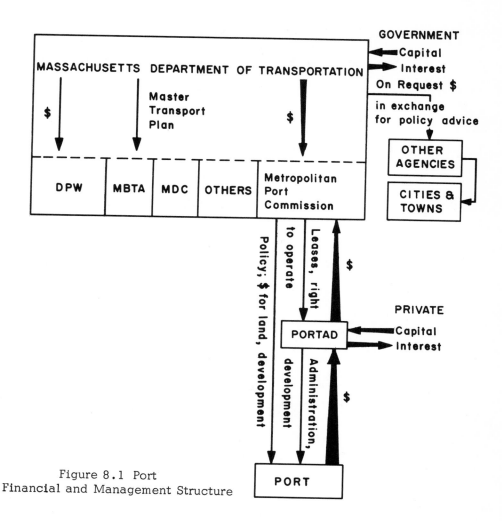

Figure 8.1 Port
Financial and Management Structure

was whether the M.P.A. presently manages the port facilities adequately, and

whether it _can_ cope with the additional facilities projected in our design. Through

personal interviews with members of the M.P.A. and the Massachusetts State

Legislature, through study of the legislation establishing the Authority[1], and

---

[1] Massachusetts General Laws, Chapter 91, Appendix Sections 1-1 to 1-39 (1969)

by comparing its mandate with those creating other state agencies (M.B.T.A.[2],
M.D.C.[3]), it was determined that the present management is ineffective and
that prospects for its future improvement appear doubtful.

The M.P.A.'s most glaring weakness has been its failure to deal with
the labor problem in the Port of Boston; apparently it cannot do so. The M.P.A.
has statutory authority to bargain collectively with its own employees, but ship
not the M.P.A. employ the dockworkers. Labor management negotiations are ca
on between the I.L.A. and the B.S.A., as previously mentioned; the M.P.A. ha
no statutory authorization to participate in these negotiations or to force a solut

Other Port Authority failings can be summed up as a lack of aggressive
management. The causes are difficult to identify, but the following have been
suggested as possible factors. First, members of the Port Authority act for it on
on a part-time, unpaid basis; they do not devote their full abilities and energy t
its management. This is not true of the M.B.T.A., and the M.D.C., both of wh
have full-time, salaried members. The difficulties of the Port of Boston and the
rapid growth of the airport would seem to demand full-time leadership of the M.
Second, the M.P.A. members are not professional port administrators. They are
influential figures from industrial firms, law offices, and unions. They do not b
expertise or even necessarily experience in port administration to the Authority.
Last, the members of the Authority feel that their primary task is to insure that p
ment is made on revenue bonds as these become due; they shy away from any inr

---

[2] Massachusetts General Laws, Chapter 161A, Sections 1-29 (1969) and Chapter
162, Appendix Sections 1-5 to 1-8, 1-21, 1-26 to 1-28 (1958).
[3] Massachusetts General Laws, Chapter 28, Section 1 and Chapter 92, Section
1-102 (1969).

vation or change involving risk. Concern for bondholders in itself is not a bad thing; in fact, it is salutory insofar as it motivates careful planning and sober judgment. However, since bondholders receive fixed return on their investment, it is improbable that they would strenuously oppose any coherent plan for development which assures sufficient revenue to meet interest and principal obligations. Satisfying bondholders or investors is an integral part of any development program and need not necessitate conservatism.

Yet even if innovation and creativity are stifled, as in the present instance, there may well be no solution which a planning group can impose on the Authority members from without. Different board members will bring different attitudes to the Authority, and if the present board is overly conservative, new members with fresh approaches can be appointed as the terms of present members expire. This issue is finally a political one, not one which planners can resolve.

Other criticism of the M.P.A. centers on its failure to bring more business to the Port of Boston and on its inability to rectify the problems of East Boston. Much of the decline of the Port derives from developments over which the M.P.A. has little or no control, as we have noted, but some portion stems from insufficient advertising and public relations. The M.P.A. is presently working to correct this. It has opened field offices in Washington, D.C., New York, Chicago, and Brussels. It sponsored a trade mission to Europe in October of 1967, bringing Boston business leaders and port officials into contact with European shippers and shipping officials. It maintains advertising schedules in selected American and European publications, and its public relations department performs numerous other incidental functions.

The problems of East Boston appear insoluable unless the airport (or most of the heavy air traffic) is moved. No satisfactory noise reduction system has been developed, and no alternative airport site has yet been announced by the M.P.A. The problem, as it now exists, given no new airport, is a political one in which the M.P.A. is caught between the legislature and the citizens of East Boston.

So, then, a lack of aggressive management, failure to achieve a port labor settlement, inadequate solicitation of port business, failure to solve the problems of East Boston, and, finally, the lack of a comprehensive plan for the future, not to mention an ultimate goal, have plagued the present M.P.A. and indicate a feeble future under present management.

## 8.2    Constraints on Port Management

Eminent domain is the right of the sovereign, the governing authority or its duly authorized agents, to appropriate the ownership and possession of private property for public use or public benefit upon payment to the owner of fair and just compensation. The general rule for individual states is that only their own constitutions limit their eminent domain power. This power may be exercised, however, only within the state's territorial boundaries, and the state legislature must prescribe the occasions, manner, and agencies for the exercise of the power. As with the Federal government, the state legislature may, by appropriate statutes, delegate its power to other agencies, and, when it does so, it may restrict the manner and extent of its use and may alter or revoke the delegated authority at any time. The statute delegating the power should so state explicitly, since it will be narrowly construed by the courts to protect the landowner from improper appropriation of his property.

Delegation may be given to public corporations and agencies such as towns and cities, port authorities, and park districts, but it must be specific; the agencies cannot take the power upon themselves simply because they fulfill a public function.

Private corporations or individuals performing public duties or serving the public good may also be permitted by the legislature to take land by eminent domain, even though they will derive a profit from their operations. The public good generated by port facilities would seem to justify giving eminent domain powers to a private port developer under suitable supervision.

Associated with the taking of land through eminent domain is the cost of compensating the land owner. The criteria for what constitutes a taking have been changing slowly. A growing number of cases have allowed recovery in suits involving airport noise. These cases hold that a continuing nuisance, such as the noise created by airplanes landing and taking off, may amount to a compensable taking. The reasoning behind these cases is as follows: when the government conducts an activity which sufficiently disturbs the use and enjoyment of neighboring land, the public should bear the cost of such activity. Also, ordinances requiring that structures above a certain height on land bordering an airport glide path be cut down or removed have been held to involve takings which require payment.

In estimating the costs of taking land, therefore, it should be kept in mind that the present limits of the government's liability for damage to property not actually taken may be enlarged if an affected landowner should decide to press suit.

The Massachusetts Port Authority possessed until recently the power of eminent domain, but political disputes with the legislature resulted in the loss of that power. The power of land taking, however, is essential to the management of a port with dynamic future plans. Therefore, the management of the new Port of Boston must have the authority of eminent domain as one of its prerequisites.

The management must deal with many other "clients" as well as with the general public neighboring on the port. It is constrained by many established traditions and laws, both written and unwritten. The port, through its management, must deal effectively with the public by providing efficient service, with the carriers by providing facilities on a par with other ports in the country, and with the government agencies such as the I.C.C. and F.A.A. by conforming to their regulations. In addition, it must provide a convenient interface for cargo transfer; it must, therefore, deal effectively with land based carriers.

## 8.3    Administration of the Port Facilities

All future development of transportation facilities in Massachusetts should be organized, planned, and to a large degree financed, with state and federal assistance, by a single Department of Transportation. The Department's primary concerns would be highways, railroads, mass transportation, and rapid transit. These are essentially intra-state facilities and since most money for their construction and operation comes directly from the

state treasury, from the federal government or from state bonds, these funds
could be distributed best through a single agency rather than through the
several agencies now concerned with different forms of transportation (the
M.B.T.A., M.D.C., D.P.W., etc.).

The Department of Transportation would exercise control in two ways.
It would take over the transportation functions of those agencies now receiving
funds directly from the state, and it would offer substantial assistance to those
communities or agencies which have their own sources of funds on the condition that they submit their plans for approval to the Department of Transportation.

The basic function of the Department of Transportation would be to draw
up and administer a Master Transportation Plan for the State of Massachusetts
and to keep the plan up to date by annual review and revision. The Master
Plan and its revisions, as they are made, would be submitted to the Governor,
who would incorporate them in an annual report to the legislature concerning
the Department and its work.

Port facilities would be, of course, part of the Massachusetts
transportation network under the general jurisdiction of the Department of
Transportation. Port planning and development, however, is concerned with
a facility qualitatively different from a highway or rapid transit system.
A port is an interface rather than a link. It requires expert management and
demands a different type of criteria than that needed to evaluate other facilities.
Among the most important differences are the following:

1) The Department of Transportation will be organized to create
and maintain an efficient network of links while the port managers

and planners must provide <u>services</u> and facilities for efficient exchange of goods within the restricted port area.

2) Ideally, a port should provide sufficient revenues to repay investors and show a profit, or at least should avoid being a public charge. A transportation network is not designed or intended to raise revenue, and the expenses of construction, maintenance, and repair are borne by the public.

3) The success of a port is measured chiefly by the volume of trade which flows through it, and it must compete with other nearby ports to maintain or increase this volume. A transportation network is judged on its efficiency and convenience and faces no competition.

Yet, in spite of these differences, a port depends on the local transportation system for a rapid flow of goods to and from the port, and any master transportation plan must reckon with the influence of changes in the port's operation upon the traffic which the master plan is designed to accommodate. High level policy decisions concerning the state's over-all economic goals will affect all transportation plans, and a single coordinating agency with one master plan will be in an excellent position to implement policy decisions without present day overlapping, duplication, or bickering. So any master plan must include plans for the port, and the port, in turn, must rely heavily on the land routes provided in the master plan to operate efficiently.

Now, how does one balance the uniqueness of port problems against the port's dependence on a master transportation plan? We have concluded that the port authorities must be attached to the Department of Transportation so as to be included in the committee developing a master plan, and they

must be bound by the plan's provisions; but they must be left free to develop

their own facilities and to operate them according to their own expert judg-

ment (subject, of course, to the supervision of the Governor and the legis-

lature).

In practice this will mean that the port authorities must participate

in formulating the master plan and subsequent amendments to it insofar as

port operations will affect transportation throughout the state. After adoption

of the master plan, the port authorities must clear with the Department of

Transportation any plans which

1) necessitate construction or substantial renovation of access

routes to the port. These projects will be undertaken and/or

financed by the Department of Transportation as if the port were

any other municipality or public body with its own sources of

revenue. If the Department of Transportation approves the project

but cannot finance it, the port authorities may petition the legis-

lature for authority to use their own funds or to acquire funds for

the purpose;

2) require the elimination or relocation of presently-existing trans-

portation facilities or traffic patterns;

3) may place substantially increased burdens on existing traffic

patterns, or threaten to seriously impede or disrupt the normal

flow of traffic in areas where present traffic is heavy or congested;

4) conflict with pre-existing local plans approved by the Department

of Transportation, but not yet carried out;

5) conflict with the Master Transportation Plan (or with amend-

ments under consideration by the Department of Transportation)

or with policy decisions which have not been formalized into

planning decisions.

What will be the criteria for passing such plans? When such a pro-

posal has been submitted by the port authorities, the Department will or

should make every reasonable effort to reconcile the proposal with any

conflicting plans and to restructure traffic patterns or construct new facilities

to deal with projected increases or changes in traffic resulting from the

proposal's implementation. If the Department of Transportation approves

the project but cannot finance any portion which it would otherwise undertake,

the port authorities may proceed to secure their own funding as we have out-

lined in 1) above. If the proposal conflicts with any local plan approved

by the Department of Transportation, but not yet under construction, the

Department may determine after a hearing that the port's proposal is necessary

and is in the public interest, and may then withdraw approval from other

inconsistent plans.

But the Department of Transportation will have no jurisdiction over

decisions relating to

1) construction or demolition of port facilities except to the extent

allowed in 3) above;

2) setting of rates and charges in the port;

3) labor-management relations;

4) construction of housing, recreational facilities, or other
projects by the port authorities except insofar as such construction affects transportation in the area surrounding it; or

5) any other decisions which do not directly affect transportation
projects or plans under the jurisdiction of the Department of
Transportation.

## 8.4    The Port Commission

The duties of developing and managing the port will be allocated
to two organizations - a public corporation to be called the Metropolitan
Port Commission, and a quasi-public corporation to be called PORTAD.
The Port Commission will be a public agency organized by the legislature
for the purposes of determining public policy for the port, acquiring and
holding title to land and certain facilities at the port, leasing land to
PORTAD for development and management, and supervising PORTAD's operations to insure conformity to policy as determined by the Port Commission
and the Department of Transportation. The Commission will consist of the
Governor or his delegate, the Mayor of Boston or his delegate, the presidents
of the Longshoremen's Union and an air transportation union, a representative
of the B.S.A. and of the air carriers, and three members of PORTAD appointed
to that body by the Governor. Figure 8.2 depicts the funding and financial
disposition of the M.P.C.

The Port Commission will have eminent domain powers and may issue
tax exempt bonds (municipal or revenue). It will work with the Department

Figure 8.2 Massachusetts Port Commission Financial Structure

of Transportation in

      1) development of the Master Transportation Plan,

      2) determination of policy for the port, and

      3) the securing of funds for certain aspects of port development for which transportation funds are available. It will make annual reports to the Governor in which it will delineate plans not covered in the Master Transportation Plan.

    The Port Commission will lease to PORTAD the port land and port facilities, and it will build and lease to PORTAD new facilities as they are needed. These leases will be the primary means by which the Commission will exercise control over the operations of PORTAD and will include provisions which allow the Commission to

      1) inspect PORTAD facilities at any time;

      2) approve schedules of rates which PORTAD will charge shippers for use of the port so as to promote port policy and to assure PORTAD a fair return on its investment;

      3) require that PORTAD submit development plans to the Port Commission for review and approval. The Commission will then

approve those plans which conform to port policy decisions

and are financially sound;

4) loan money to PORTAD upon such terms and conditions as

will most effectively carry out the policies of the port;

5) terminate the lease if at any time PORTAD fails to abide by

policies drawn up by the Port Commission and approved by the

Department of Transportation.

## 8.5     PORTAD

PORTAD (Figure 8.3) will be organized as a private corporation and

financed by private capital. It will issue stock as well as bonds (non tax-

exempt). 50% of the stock will be reserved for purchase by the carriers

who use the port, and 50% will be issued for purchase by the general public.

Each half of the total stock issue will elect 6 members to the Board of

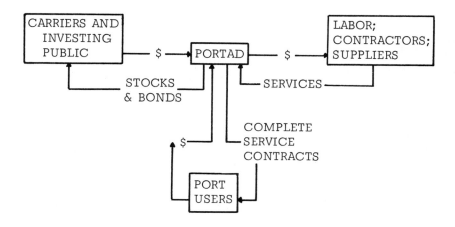

Figure 8.3 PORTAD Structure and Financing

Governors of PORTAD, and 3 other members will be appointed by the Governor

and will serve ex officio on the Massachusetts Port Commission. The Board

of Governors will perform the same functions as do the board of directors of

any private corporation.

PORTAD will be responsible for effecting the policies of the Port

Commission and for developing and operating all facilities. It will secure

its own financing for its projects, except insofar as the Port Commission

may contribute capital or facilities. It will operate under the supervision

of the Port Commission at all times, but the Commission shall not interfere

with its operations unless those operations threaten the implementation of

important port policy or materially impair the efficiency or value of the port.

The execution of the integrated port area plan will be the joint responsibilities

of the Department of Transportation, the Port Commission, and PORTAD.

PORTAD will supply all services to port users and will charge reason-

able fees therefore. It will deal directly with stevedoring companies who,

in turn, will hire the longshoremen. Negotiations for labor contracts will

be carried on by the longshoremen , the stevedoring companies, and PORTAD.

All procurement will be handled by PORTAD and when PORTAD itself cannot

provide certain related services, it will contract them out, so that it can

offer a single contract to users covering all service and use charges. At

airport facilities, PORTAD may also choose to provide a single contract for

users or it may enter into sub-leases with the carriers who wish to build

their own terminals; in any case, it will be left free to adopt any feasible

scheme.

## 8.6    Coordination of Port Administration

By this blending of private and public control in the port we hope to

1) deal with the labor problem in the port;

2) encourage innovation and modern business practices in the port's operation by means of a profit incentive;

3) offer the investing public several different investment alternatives, thereby making it easer to raise the large amount of capital necessary for the major renovation proposed by Project BOSPORUS;

4) encourage PORTAD's continual updating of port facilities by making available to it, as a tax-paying individual, the tax shelter available through construction and renovation of depreciable property.

The dangers we must guard against are

1) duplication and delay in planning because of the many agencies involved and the requirement of a master plan which must reconcile conflicting interests;

2) hindering of developments within the port through inertia, or priorities, or through opposition in the Department of Transportation, over which the port authorities will have little or no control.

We believe that we have built into our proposal sufficient flexibility to deal with the first of these problems if it should arise. The second problem is a calculated risk which we believe should be taken because we feel that coordination of transportation planning is an end to be desired. We also

feel that the present opposition to the Massachusetts Port Authority in the

General Court (which has brought about a limitation of the Authority's emi-

nent domain power and may place further restrictions on its operations)

could be removed or diminished by associating the port development plans

with a comprehensive statewide transportation plan.

## 8.7    Funding of the Port Facility

Large amounts of capital are generally difficult and costly to obtain.

Consequently, a scheme has been devised to raise the capital at lower

costs than by the usual methods. For the purpose of this scheme, it is

assumed that the funds given by the federal, state, and local government

agencies will be obtained through the proper channels and that we are

confronted with raising $300 million in order to construct the remaining

facilities.

The organizational structure outlined in 8.4 and 8.5 was created

for the purpose of involving the private sector, thereby increasing the pro-

fitability potential of the port, as well as minimizing the annual interest

payments on bonds or debt equities. The funding will take place in two

stages. First, $150 million will be raised for the use of the Massachusetts

Port Commission. This money, supplemented by the profits from the sale

of presently owned land, will provide adequate funds for the acquisition of

land and for non-government supported construction. After the land has been

acquired and whatever basic construction requirements have been fulfilled,

the M.P.C. will lease the land and its attachments to PORTAD. PORTAD

will then seek funding on its own, one to two years after the initial funding
of the M.P.C. The M.P.C. will pay an interest rate of 5% on its municipal
bonds which means that it must receive at least $7.5 million annually. This
money must be earned by operations of the port, via the leasing arrangements
with PORTAD.

PORTAD will require approximately $150 million and will raise the
money by issuing the following: 1) $15 million in bonds at an annual interest
rate of 6.5%; 2) a convertible preferred stock of $60 million, designated pri-
marily for the carriers or institutional investors at 2% cash divident and 3%
stock divident annually; 3) finally, a common stock issue of $75 million to

## Massachusetts Port Commission

### 1970
$150 million - municipal bonds at 5%; annual interest $7.5 million

## PORTAD

### 1971-72
$150 million
  1) $15 million - bonds at 6.5%; annual interest $975,000
  2) $60 million - convertible preferred stock at 2% cash,
     3% stock dividend; annual dividend $1.2 million; annual
     dilution $1.8 million
  3) $75 million - common stock, no dividend

  Issue warrants with common stock to obtain one share stock
  for each 20 shares at 20% above market. Also issue rights
  to purchase stock on annual basis to shareholders to raise
  capital.

Figure 8.4 Port Development Funding

be spread over a period of approximately 5 years. A warrant to the investors

to purchase 1 share of common stock for each 20 shares held at issue, at

a price of 20% above issue price, good for 10 years, will compensate for

the loss of dividends. In addition, a yearly stock rights offering to share-

holders on record as of a specified date, to buy common stock at some reduced

price, would be an added appeal to investors. By this technique one can also

procure money to pay off any debts on senior securities which might not other-

wise be met because of insufficient operating revenues. The outline in Figure

8.4 provides a quick view of our funding plan.

Chapter 9

BOSPORUS TIME LINE

In Chapters 5 through 8 the Bosporus plan laid out in Chapter 1
is divided into units devoted to "the airport", "the seaport", "labor", and
"port management". The airport and seaport chapters discuss the facilities
in some detail and briefly sketch the stages of development which could
lead to a complete, integrated system by 1990. This chapter outlines
specifically the sequence of seaport and airport consolidation, alteration,
and construction which would culminate in the proposed Bosporus design.
A brief conclusion terminates the chapter and the report.

## 9.1    The Design Time Line

The 1969 Longshoremen's contract in which labor agreed to handle
containerized shipments has set the stage for the first step toward the completed system: the opening of Castle Island to general shipping. First, however,
two further measures must be taken. Negotiations with Sea-Land, Inc. to obtain
the container crane and the lease to the Island must be successfully undertaken.
More essentially, the management structure (the M.D.T., M.P.C., and PORTAD)
outlined in Chapter 8 must be created. Let us hypothesize that laws to establish

the M.D.T. and M.P.C. are passed by the Massachusetts Legislature in

1970 and that appropriate funds are at the same time delegated to these agencies.

Let us assume the enthusiastic formation of PORTAD as a quick response to

this government action. Castle Island might then begin operation in 1970;

modification and construction of new container cranes would progress concurrent-

ly with operation for one year. The Island would then be in full use in 1971.

To return to labor, from 1970 until the system achieves a steady state

in 1990, the semi-retirement plan or possibly other labor plans described in

Chapter 7 would be implemented. The choice of plans and their application would

be determined by the extent of automation and of port use in these years.

New construction of container facilities at the Army Base would also

begin in 1970. By 1971-72, operations at Castle Island and the Army Base would

permit a 30% cut back in general shipping operations elsewhere in the Harbor,

freeing land in East Boston, Charlestown, and South Boston. By 1974, the

Army Base would be operating at 80% capacity and an additional 30% cut back

would take place. By 1976 the Army Base would be used to 100% capacity.

Finally, 1970 would see the first steps toward an Inner Harbor freeing of

shipping facilities. To keep oil tankers from the Inner Harbor, oil pipelines from

the Chelsea Creek tank farms to oil terminals in the Outer Harbor would be built

from 1970 to 1972. From 1970 to 1981 tank farms would be moved in stages from

the lower end of Chelsea Creek to the upper Creek. Finally, a bulk cargo

unloading buoy would be built at some time in the 70's relieving the Harbor of

further shipping traffic. Depollution projects would generally accompany

consolidation and removal of general shipping facilities in the Harbor.

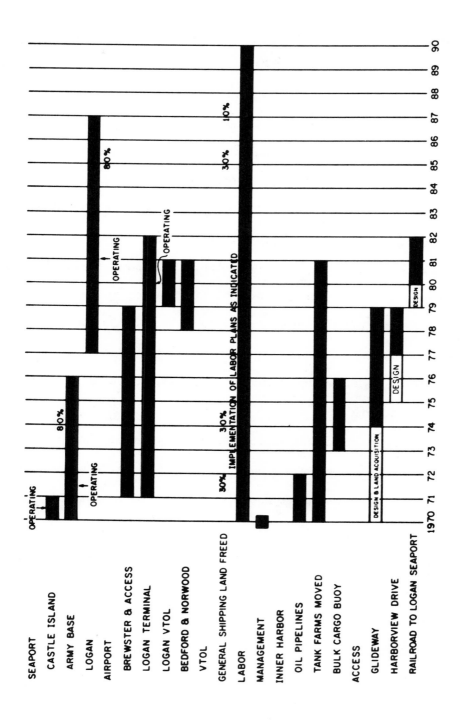

Figure 9.1 BOSPORUS Time Line

At Logan, the key site in the total seaport-airport development, air terminal alterations would begin in 1971. Construction of the Brewster jetport would begin at the same time. Eight years later, in 1979, Brewster and its access route would be complete and Logan would act as the Brewster terminal. With Logan freed of jet traffic, some land would be free for industrial or other development, while full construction of the Logan seaport facilities could now take place. (Two years earlier, in 1977, preliminary seaport work not interfering with the active runways would have begun.)

In 1978, construction of the two outlying VTOL ports at Bedford and Norwood would begin. A year later work on the VTOL port at Logan would be begun and all three would be completed and open in 1981. By 1982 the Logan terminal would be finished, completing the transformation of Logan's air operations from complete jet service to merely terminal operations and to a VTOL-general aviation port.

Construction of Logan's seaport facilities would progress at the rate of three berths a year until in 1985 the facilities would be 80-90% complete. At this time another 30% cut back in general shipping operations elsewhere in the Harbor would occur. In 1987 Logan would be complete and at that time the last 10% cut back would occur. All public general cargo shipping would now involve Logan, Castle Island, or the Army Base. Although private shipping facilities would continue to operate in the Harbor, citizen pressure, legislative regulation, and the good example set by the shipping operations at M.P.C. facilities might spur other operators to similarly consolidate and update their facilities. Therefore, additional land might revert to the city or private developers

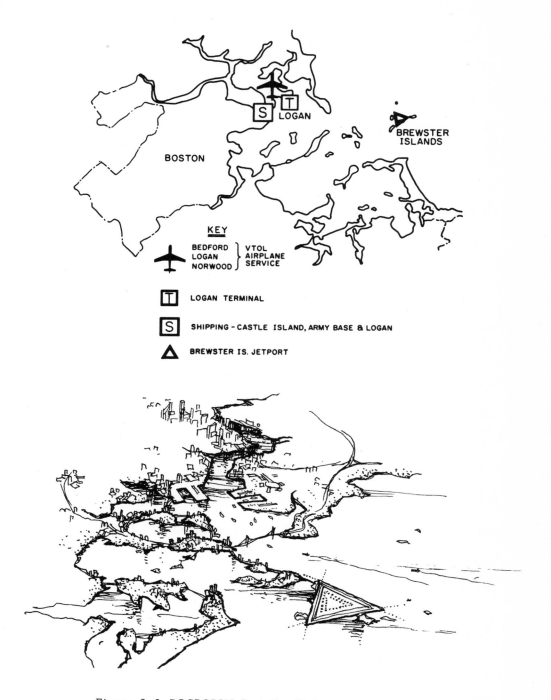

Figure 9.2 BOSPORUS Port Facilities in Boston Harbor

and a more extensive improvement in the Harbor could result.

The access systems described in Chapter 5 would be constructed simultaneously with the actual port facilities. Design and land acquisition for the Glideway System would take place from 1970 to 1974; actual construction would progress from 1974 until 1979. The Glideway system would therefore (by design) begin operation at the same time as the Brewster jetport. Completion of the Norwood and Bedford Glideway terminals might be delayed if necessary until the 1981 opening of these VTOL ports.

From 1975 to 1977, the Harborview Drive would be designed and construction could follow from 1977 to 1979 if it did not interfere with Brewster access construction. At all events, construction would take two years and would depend upon the existence of shared portions of the Brewster access link. Last, the removal of the railroad tracks and terminal from East Boston to the Logan seaport could be planned from 1979 to 1980 and carried out from 1980 to 1982, the time at which they would be needed.

By 1990, the target date for our design, all components of the system would be in "steady state". Figure 9.1 is a time line showing the staging of the entire Bosporus plan as discussed above. Figure 9.2 illustrates the BOSPORUS airport and seaport facilities in the Harbor. Figure 9.3 is a close-up of Harbor shipping facilities.

9.2    Final Words

An examination of the problems encountered by city after city across the country in meeting the demands for adequate modern transportation facilities

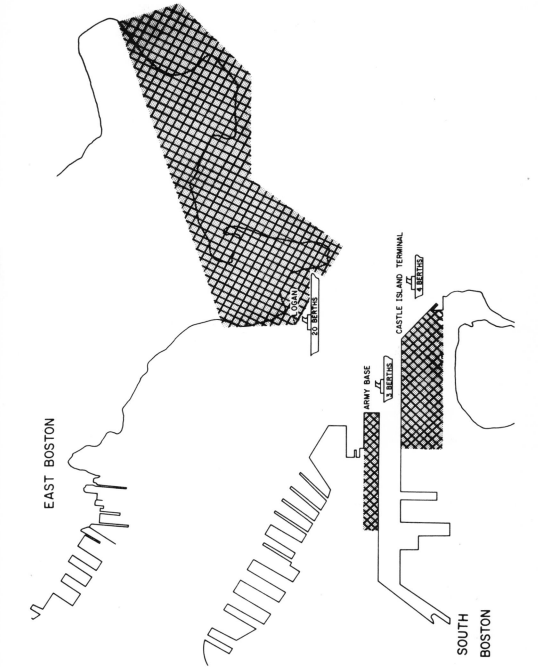

Figure 9.3 BOSPORUS Seaport Facilities

amply demonstrates the difficulties that result from focusing attention on too narrow a segment of the problem. Believing that past attempts to improve Boston's port facilities have suffered from this same shortcoming, we attempted to undertake as broad a study of the needs and alternatives facing Boston as we could.

Our first decision was to examine both the airport and the seaport simultaneously. We then looked at present utilization of facilities and at projected demands. We examined alternatives for meeting and influencing demand in the light of projected technological developments, locational alternatives, institutional possibilities, and citizen reactions. We believe that implementation of the plan outlined would represent a significant step toward providing Boston with the transportation facilities that will be needed to secure its future position as one of America's great cities. The plans may be considered too bold, but we believe that only through the implementation of bold plans can the needs of the future be met.

Finally, although the plans outlined here relate specifically to the Boston situation, the methodology is generally applicable and we hope that the presentation of these results will lead others to undertake comparably broad studies of the needs of other specific areas.